DEEP
DIVER
MANUAL

PADI®
padi.com

_____

Student Diver

_____

Address

_____

City, State/Province

_____

Telephone

_____   _____

Instructor   *Date*

PADI Members are licensed to use various PADI Trademarks and to conduct PADI training. Individual, dive center and resort Members are not agents, employees or franchisees of PADI. Member business activities are independent, and are neither owned nor operated by PADI. While PADI establishes the standards for PADI diver training programs, it is not responsible for, nor does it have the right to control, the operation of the Members' business activities and the day-to-day conduct of PADI programs and supervision of divers by the Members or their associated staff.

Deep Diver *Manual*

Published by PADI
30151 Tomas
Rancho Santa Margarita, CA 92688-2125

ISBN 978-1-878663-44-3

Printed in Canada

Product No. 79300 (Rev. 04/19) Version 2.01

Table of Contents

DEEP
DIVER
MANUAL

PADI
padi.com

_____

Student Diver

_____

Address

_____

City, State/Province

_____

Telephone

_____   _____

Instructor   *Date*

PADI Members are licensed to use various PADI Trademarks and to conduct PADI training. Individual, dive center and resort Members are not agents, employees or franchisees of PADI. Member business activities are independent, and are neither owned nor operated by PADI. While PADI establishes the standards for PADI diver training programs, it is not responsible for, nor does it have the right to control, the operation of the Members' business activities and the day-to-day conduct of PADI programs and supervision of divers by the Members or their associated staff.

Deep Diver *Manual*

Published by PADI
30151 Tomas
Rancho Santa Margarita, CA 92688-2125

ISBN 978-1-878663-44-3

Printed in Canada

Product No. 79300 (Rev. 04/19) Version 2.01

Table of Contents

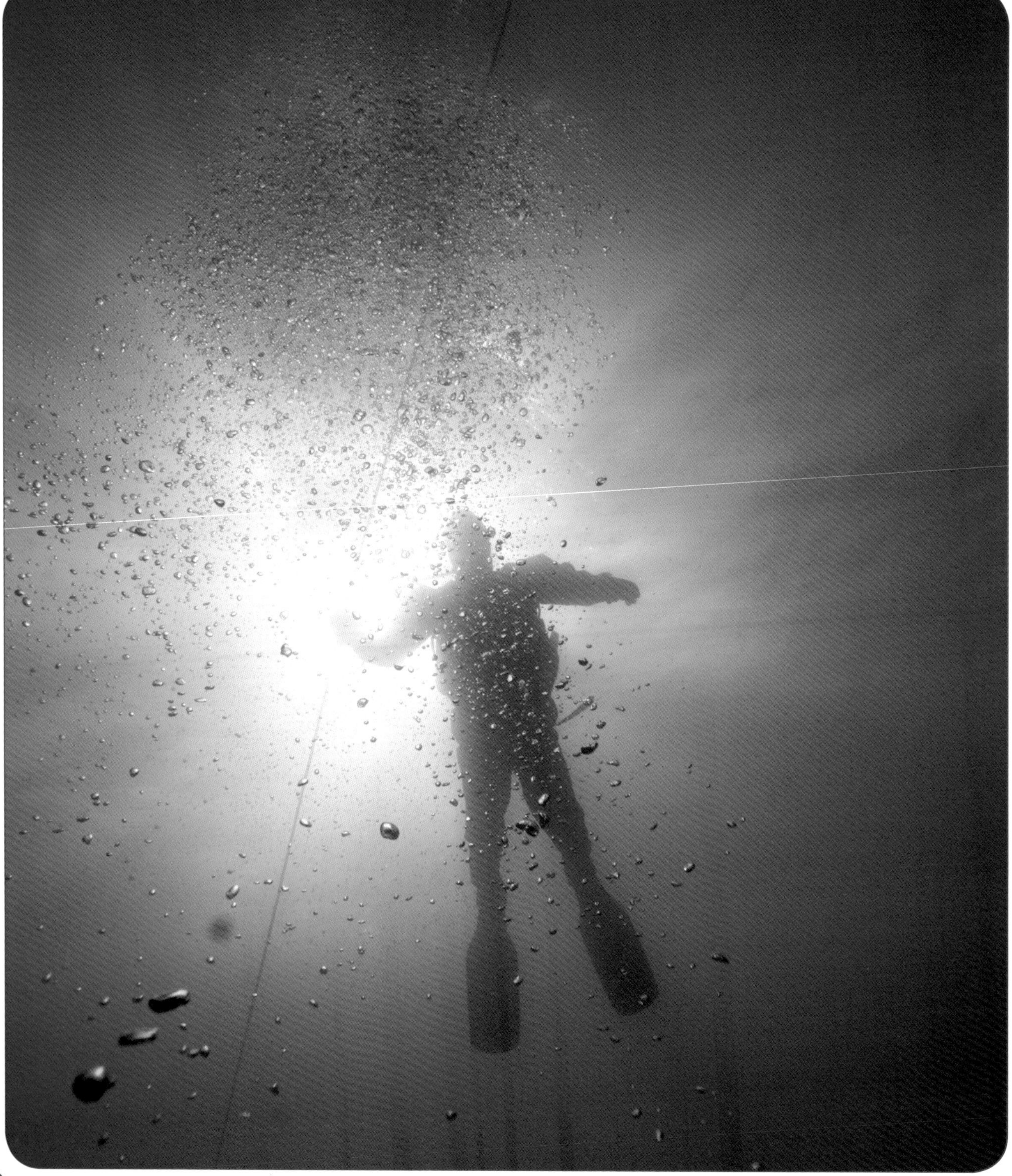

Introduction

Like Sirens, the depths seduce us, and like Ulysses, we go. Coral walls and sapphire water tempt us to descend just a bit more, then more, then . . . . Deep-water wrecks entice us, calling us to explore them. Sometimes the depth lures us simply because it is there.

It's a rare diver who hasn't felt the urge to dive deep. As a general rule, divers tend to be adventurous people, and deep diving - whether to visit a wreck or take photos - can certainly be called adventurous. It's only natural that like most divers, you have some interest in deep diving.

It's common sense that with greater depths come more potential hazards. However, not all deep diving hazards are obvious; the untrained and unaware diver may not recognize them. Proper deep diving techniques manage these hazards, but even trained recreational deep divers face unacceptable risk if they descend below reasonable limits.

The PADI Deep Diver Specialty course teaches you the techniques that make recreational deep diving safe and fun. You'll learn deep diving limits, and how to stay within them. Your skill and ability as a diver will improve as you practice deep diving techniques. You'll find that PADI Deep Diver training opens the doors to new dive sites and new adventure, especially when combined with other interests like underwater photography, wreck diving or observing underwater organisms.

Course Overview

As in most PADI Specialty Diver courses, the PADI Deep Diver course emphasizes diving, and you will make at least four deep dives in open water with your PADI Instructor. You'll have fun on these dives while developing and refining the skills you need for deep diving.

The course includes the background information that you'll apply during deep dives as well as practical skills you'll demonstrate. Normally you'll cover this information by reading this manual, by watching the PADI *Deep Diving* video, and by discussing the material with your instructor prior to your dives. Your instructor may decide to have more formal class meetings. The recommended sequence is to begin by skimming through this manual, noting the headings, topics and pictures. This speeds learning by giving you an idea of where you're headed. Then, as your read, highlight or underline the answers to the study objectives. **It's important to actually do this** - not simply note them - because the physical act of writing/highlighting enhances transferring the knowledge to long term memory. Answer the exercises, reviewing anything you don't understand. Then, fill out the Knowledge Reviews to turn in to your instructor.

PADI Deep Diver Course Prerequisites

To take the PADI Deep Diver course, you must be certified as a PADI Adventure Diver or have a qualifying certification from another training organization similar to that of a PADI Advanced Open Water Diver.

After completing the manual, watch the *Deep Diving* video. This reinforces what you read, and shows demonstrations of many of the skills you'll learn. If you prefer to watch the video first, that's fine.

You may initially practice some of the skills you'll learn in controlled conditions, such as at the surface, or in pool or confined water. Your instructor may add dives for added time to develop and refine your skills, and for fun.

When you've completed the course, you'll have earned the PADI Deep Diver certification, which qualifies you to deep dive in conditions comparable to or better than those in which you have experience and training. With your PADI Deep Diver certification, you can apply for the Master Scuba Diver rating if you also have the PADI Rescue Diver certification, and four other PADI specialty certifications.

The PADI Deep Diver certification credits toward the PADI Master Scuba Diver rating - recreational diving's highest nonprofessional level.

Important

 While you can learn many aspects of deep diving by reading this manual and watching the video, it doesn't replace hands-on learning with your PADI Instructor.

Other Skills You'll Want as a PADI Deep Diver

Deep diving integrates well with the skills you develop in new opportunities through training in other PADI Specialty Diver courses.

- **PADI Enriched Air Diver** - Enriched air nitrox extends your no stop times, which can be particularly handy when conducting deep dives in the 18 metre/60 foot to 30 metre/100 foot depth range. Enriched air maximizes your no stop dive time, and can especially benefit how long you can make repetitive dives after an initial deep dive.

- **PADI Wreck Diver** - Also, because wrecks tend to be deeper dives, wreck diving and deep diving often go hand-in-hand. In many areas, you'll do your PADI Deep Diver course and PADI Wreck Diver course on the same wrecks.

- **PADI Digital Underwater Photographer** - One of the motivations for deep diving is to see things and go places you don't find on shallower dives. It's fun to capture images of your deep dives to share with others, but with little time on a deep dive and the extra procedures you apply, photography needs to be second nature if you want good results. This course builds photo skills so you can get the shots you want while deep diving appropriately.

- **PADI Dry Suit Diver** - Deep diving is often in cool to cold water because deeper water tends to be colder. In addition, wet suits compress with depth and lose their insulating abilities, whereas shell dry suits lose little of their insulating qualities with depth. Certification as a PADI Dry Suit Diver prepares you to visit deeper dives more comfortably.

- **PADI Peak Performance Buoyancy Diver** - It's useful to fine tune your buoyancy skills. Good buoyancy control helps you to control your descents and ascents to and from depth, to perform safety stops at 5 metres/15 feet before surfacing without physically holding on to a reference line for positioning, and to minimize incidental contact with your surroundings helping you protect sensitive marine organisms or fragile parts of shipwrecks.

- **DSAT TecRec** - If you find your interest in deep diving creates a strong interest in making longer dives that require decompression stops, or dives below recreation depth limits, you may be interested in becoming a tec diver. If you're interested in this kind of diving, having the proper training and equipment is mandatory.

The first dive of most PADI specialties* corresponds to the same dive in the PADI Adventures in Diving program. Therefore, if you're a PADI Advanced Open Water Diver or Adventure Diver, you're already made the first dive in these specialty courses. Similarly, the first dive of the specialties credits toward the Advanced Open Water Diver or Adventure Diver certification.

Successfully completing five PADI Specialties and the PADI Rescue Diver course qualifies you for the PADI Master Scuba Diver rating - the highest nonprofessional rating in the sport.

For more information about PADI courses, including specialties, the Adventures in Diving program and PADI Master Scuba Diver, visit padi.com.

Watch for These Symbols

 Alerts you to important safety information. Pay close attention when you see this symbol and consult your instructor if you do not understand the material.

 This Project A.W.A.R.E. symbol highlights information or a specific diving technique that allows you to interact harmoniously with the aquatic environment.

 Alerts you to additional/related information on PADI videos, books, CD-ROM and other media. This material is for your interest and further learning. The information required for this course is in this manual.

*PADI Ice Diver, Cavern Diver, Semiclosed Rebreather, and TecRec courses do not have corresponding dives in the Adventures in Diving program.

Why *Dive Deep?*

Deep Diving Activities

As you may remember from your PADI Advanced Open Water Diver course, deep diving is a means to an end.

You make a deep dive to see, to do or to experience something that you can't on a shallower dive. There's no reason to make a deep dive if you can make essentially the same dive at a shallower depth.

Being certified as a PADI Deep Diver gives you access to new dive sites and activities. In some resort areas, in fact, you may find that the majority of the popular dive sites are deep dives; this is especially true in areas known for large, relatively intact shipwrecks. Therefore, you'll want to be familiar with the knowledge, equipment, skills and techniques of deep diving so you can visit these sites.

You'll find as many deep diving activities as there are sites and interests. The possibilities are endless, but here are some examples:

Observing aquatic life or topography.

In both freshwater and saltwater environments, you can find organisms in deeper water that don't live, or are

Study Objective

Underline/highlight the answers to these questions as you read:

1. What are five reasons to deep dive?

2. What is the difference between a proper and an improper deep diving objective?

less common, in shallow water. In freshwater, catfish, carp, trout and other fish tend to be found deeper - especially during the day. In the ocean, many black corals, including black coral bull kelp, and varieties of sponges can only be found in deep water.

Waves, boat anchors, fishing and other potentially negative influences tend to affect deep areas less than shallow ones, so deep diving often lets you observe the aquatic organisms in a less changed environment. Often deep sites are found where land meets open ocean, making them ideal for spotting pelagic animals that don't frequent reefs.

Specific topography tends to be associated with deep water. Walls usually rise out of impressive depths, even if they reach near the surface. Pinnacles and seamounts are the tops of oceanic mountains tall enough to nearly reach the surface, and tend to be great deep dive sites.

Deep diving allows you to observe aquatic life that doesn't live or isn't as common at a shallower depth. Often, deeper environments are more pristine than their shallower counterparts because storms and waves affect them less.

Exploring wrecks.

Although you can find many shallow water wrecks, by far, you'll find more in deep water - primarily because ships are big. One reason is that large ships on oceans and major lakes cruise in deeper water to avoid navigational hazards such as reefs or other obstacles. Therefore, when an accident sinks a major ship, often it happens in deep water.

Deep diving on wrecks has some advantages. In many environments, deep wrecks lie untouched by waves, surge and ice that more quickly rip apart shallow ones. The cool, lower-oxygen water common to some deep sites preserves wrecks, too. Deep freshwater wrecks have been found with paint intact after more than 100 years submerged.

Learn more *see the PADI* Wreck Diver Manual

Taking pictures.

Besides seeing deep water organisms, a wreck, or other deep site, if you're an underwater photographer, you may want photographs, too. You can take pictures you won't get in shallow water, but underwater photography in deep water requires some extra considerations.

For example, some submersible snapshot cameras won't stand up to much pressure; be sure to use a camera rated for the depth. In addition, water absorbs light, removing reds, oranges and yellows as you descend. This means deep underwater photography almost always requires a submersible flash and effective use of the white balance control. As mentioned earlier, as a general rule, deep underwater photography calls for greater familiarity with your equipment so you use time effectively and don't lose sight of deep diving procedures. You can learn more about these in the PADI Digital Underwater Photographer course.

Learn more *see* The PADI Digital Underwater Photographer Manual

---

Responsible Wreck Diving Considerations

Shipwrecks offer adventure and are often included among the best dive sites in the world. Divers must be responsible when exploring these submerged sites, looking after themselves, the environment and the cultural heritage. It's important to adhere to special considerations:

1. Respect the Heritage and Loss

2. Respect the Environment

3. Respect Others

4. Respect Your Limitations

5. Respect the Law

6. Respect Safety

7. Respect the History and Archeology

You can download the complete *Project AWARE Foundation* brochure *"Responsible Wreck Diving Considerations"* located at http://www.projectaware.org/americas/english/rwdc.asp .

It's rewarding to take photos on deep dives, but you'll want to be completely familiar with taking photos so you can use time effectively while following deep diving procedures and minimize any potential for incidental contact with the objects of your photos.

10 Tips for Underwater Photographers

Deep dives offer adventure and are often included among the best dive sites in the world to take photographs. Underwater photography in deep water requires some extra considerations. Divers must be responsible when photographing deep-water organisms, looking after themselves, and the environment. It's important to adhere to these tips:

1. Photograph with Care
2. Dive Neutral
3. Resist Temptation
4. Easy Does It
5. Sharpen Your Skills

6. Be Informed
7. Be an AWARE Diver
8. Take Only Pictures, Leave Only Bubbles
9. Share Your Images
10. Conserve the Adventure

You can download the complete *Project AWARE Foundation* brochure *"10 Tips for Underwater Photographers"* located at http://www.projectaware.org/americas/english/pdfs/10tipsUnderWaterPhoto.pdf .

Drift diving.

When strong currents rush over a dive site, drift diving poses an attractive alternative to fighting the water: float along with it, relax and watch the scenery flow by. Some of the best dive destinations, such as Cozumel, Maldives, Mexico, Palau and West Palm Beach, Florida, U.S.A., are recognized for spectacular drift diving.

Much drift diving occurs in prevailing oceanic currents, which slow or stop in shallow water. Therefore, drift diving frequently involves deep diving along walls or along reefs.

Learn more *see the PADI* Adventures in Diving Manual

Recovering objects.

If you enjoy bottom combing or search and recovery diving, your search may take you into deep water. After all, your target is where it is, not where you'd necessarily choose for it to be.

To account for short bottom times and rapid air use, deep-water search and recovery applies close teamwork, thorough planning and attention to detail. Deep-water recoveries that require lift bags and other specialized recovery techniques fall beyond the scope of this course. It's recommended that you become certified as a PADI Search and Recovery Diver, as well as a Deep Diver, before attempting them.

Learn more *see the PADI* Search and Recovery Diver Manual

Objectives

It's clear that you can find many reasons to make a deep dive. However, unlike shallower dives, deep dives tend to be short – you don't have time to do much because you have short no decompression limits and use your air more rapidly. Therefore, you need to decide what your objective is – what it is you want to accomplish on the dive – before you go.

A proper deep diving objective will be nearly singular and specific, such as to explore part of a wreck or reef, observe or photograph a particular type organism, visit striking features such as a coral tunnel, or participate in training. "Go see what is there" is often all you can expect to do on a deep dive.

Some divers can accomplish more than others in a given situation, but the idea is to minimize stress and avoid task loading by attempting no more than you can reasonable expect to accomplish. If you select a complicated objective that is more than you can realistically expect to do, you have set an *improper* deep diving objective.

About Thrills and Personal Records

Somewhere in your dive experience or training, you may have been told "A thrill isn't a good reason to go deep diving," or "Don't dive deep just to set a personal record." Don't ignore the important safety message this recommendation carries with it. However, as a PADI Deep Diver, realize there's a difference between diving for the adventure and diving for thrill seeking.

There's no question that deep diving can be exciting and thrilling. Adventure is one reason diving is fun – for many people, it's the main reason they dive. Therefore, it follows that deep diving purely for the excitement can be a valid reason for a dive. If you're properly equipped and trained, and observe the appropriate limits, there's nothing unreasonable about deep diving for the thrill of the experience. On the other hand, deep diving without proper equipment or training and exceeding appropriate limits as a thrill seeker facing risk is the kind of behavior that leads to accidents and injuries – with often fatal results.

There's nothing wrong with gaining deep diving experience by progressively and sensibly working to greater depths. If you do this with proper equipment and training, and within appropriate and accepted limits, there's nothing unreasonable about tracking and logging your progress as you gain experience and reach for greater depths. By contrast, making deep

A proper deep diving objective will be nearly singular and specific, such as "see what is there."

dives well beyond your training, equipment capabilities, or pushing personal limits just for the thrill, can have fatal consequences.

There's nothing wrong with deep diving for the excitement of it or to extend your experience into deeper water, provided that you do so responsibly. You do that by sticking to the limits and applying the techniques you learn in the PADI Deep Diver Specialty course.

Exercise 1 – Why Deep Dive?

1. Activities that you may enjoy while deep diving includes (check all that apply):
   ☐ a. drift diving.
   ☐ b. photography.
   ☐ c. observing aquatic life or striking underwater features.
   ☐ d. wreck diving.

2. A proper deep diving objective typically includes several tasks so you accomplish a lot in the short time available.
   ☐ True   ☐ False

How'd you do?
1. a, b, c, d. 2. False. A proper deep diving objective is nearly singular because you don't have time to accomplish much.

What is a Deep Dive?

Definition of a Deep Dive

As a diver qualified to take the PADI Deep Diver Specialty course, you probably already know that a recreational deep dive is generally defined as a dive deeper than 18 metres/60 feet to an absolute maximum depth limit of 40 metres/130 feet. Picking a particular depth to define "deep" or set a limit might seem arbitrary, but for more than four decades, these have proved useful and reliable guides. The recreational diving community accepts both nearly universally.

Study Objectives

Underline/highlight the answers to these questions as you read:

1. What's the definition of a recreational deep dive?

2. What are four reasons that 30 metres/100 feet is recommended as the optimal depth limit for recreational diving?

3. What five factors should you consider when setting your personal depth limit?

Although your maximum depth limit as a PADI Deep Diver is 40 metres/130 feet, you'll probably find 30 metres/100 feet your *optimum* limit for most deep dives. First, you have little time below 30 metres/100 feet, even though you'll probably use a dive computer and enriched air nitrox to allow more no stop time (especially when you use both). Computers expand your dive time when you multilevel dive (see "Using Computers" in the Deep Diving Equipment section for more about multilevel diving), and EANx reduces the amount of nitrogen in your breathing gas. Nevertheless, your time gets significantly shorter below 30 metres/100 feet because you're consuming air/EANx faster, shortening your overall dive. You have to watch your computer closely so you begin your ascent well within no stop limits, and you have to watch the depth limits of the EANx blends you can use, due to oxygen toxicity concerns.

Second, at approximately 30 metres/100 feet some divers begin to experience the first effects of nitrogen narcosis. Although narcosis doesn't heavily affect most people at these depths, staying shallower helps avoid the problem. Third, dives below 30 metres/100 feet have some additional risk of decompression sickness (DCS), primarily because it's much easier to accidentally "push" or even exceed the no stop limits, even with a single cylinder. If you end up requiring emergency decompression, you might not have enough air to complete the emergency stop (more about this later).

Finally, light reduces as you go deeper. Although clear water environments may have adequate light deeper than you can dive, in more temperate environments light falls off dramatically at about 30 metres/100 feet and aquatic life thins out. This makes it harder to see, and there's less to see anyway. In yet other environments, particularly many freshwater lakes, light may fall off or be completely blocked even shallower than 30 metres/100 feet.

Beyond the PADI Deep Diver Course

Diving deeper than 40 metres/130 feet calls for requirements beyond recreational deep diving. Although the PADI Deep Diver course provides the foundation you need for moving into tec diving (in fact, it's a requirement), you need considerably more equipment and training for tec diving.

Typical Tec Diver Equipment

- Twin cylinders - 12 litre/120 cubic feet or larger cylinder

    - Mask and power fins

    - Twin independent high-performance regulators, one with 2 m/7 ft second stage hose

    - Dual isolator manifold

    - One or more decompression cylinders with EANx and/or oxygen

    - Full wet suit or dry suit

    - Plate or fabric harness, BCD and backup BCD with low-pressure inflators

    - Weight system

    - 2 ways to monitor depth, time and decompression requirements

    - Compass

- Reel and lift bag

- Primary and backup dive knives/line cutters

- Equipment weight: 55 - 110 kg/120 - 220 lbs

Learn more...

DSAT Tec Deep Diver Course

Through a balanced mix of independent study, classroom discussion, and surface, pool and open water training exercises, the Tec Deep Diver course provides the knowledge and skills you need to become an entry-level technical deep diver.

In the Tec Deep Diver course, you learn the techniques and procedures required for diving beyond the recreational limits, making planned staged decompression dives, and using multiple gas blends on a single dive. You will find this to be one of the most extensive and intensive courses you've taken, though one of the most exhilarating. Because the Tec Deep Diver course must establish the wide foundational skill/knowledge base you need as a tec diver, it is a relatively long program. For flexibility, there are subdivisions within the Tec Deep Diver course (Tec Diver Level 1 and Tec Basics) that give you the option to complete the program in stages.

Learn more *see* The PADI Tec Deep Diver Manual

Learn more...

DSAT Tec Trimix Diver Course

For the tec diver ready to explore the outer edges of technical deep diving, the gas of choice is *trimix* - a gas blend consisting of oxygen, helium and nitrogen. The DSAT Tec Trimix Diver course is designed for individuals already certified and experienced in technical deep decompression diving with air, enriched air nitrox and oxygen.

The Tec Trimix Diver course builds upon the skills in the Tec Deep Diver course (you should have these mastered *before* you begin using helium breathing gases) taking you below 50 metres/165 feet. Trimix, which offsets narcosis and oxygen toxicity, opens the door to pristine dive sites few divers - if any - ever see. However, helium adds complexity to the dive by requiring special decompression procedures and being less forgiving of procedural errors.

Tec diving isn't for everyone, but if it interests you, ask your PADI Instructor or visit padi.com to learn more about the DSAT Tec Deep Diver course and other TecRec programs. The TecRec course series is the most comprehensive and instructionally valid tec diver training available.

Learn more *see* The PADI Tec Trimix Diver Manual

Personalizing Your Depth Limit

The established 30 metre/100 foot and 40 metre/130 foot limits (optimum and maximum) set the outside boundaries for general deep diving, but when you deep dive, you need to revise these limits based on yourself, your buddy and the environment. In other words, just because you *could* go to a certain depth doesn't mean you *should*.

Consider two dives to 27 metres/90 feet, one in clear, currentless tropical water, and the other in murky, cold water in a strong current. Even a relatively inexperienced deep diver could plan and make the first dive, but the second might call for experience with limited visibility, current lines and dry suits, in addition to deep diver training. Even if you are capable of the latter dive but hadn't been diving for a while, you'd want to refresh your underwater skills before making such a dive.

As a PADI Deep Diver, it's your responsibility to set a realistic depth limit by asking yourself some questions about five factors:

1. Environment

What is the visibility? The less visibility, the less light there is at depth. What is the temperature? In a wet suit, and/ or if there's one or more thermoclines you'll be colder at depth. Are there currents or water motion? These make you breathe faster, depleting your air supply more quickly.

In personalizing your depth limit, consider the visibility, temperature, water motion and other environmental effects.

What is the altitude? Altitude diving calls for special procedures that adjust the actual depth to a theoretical depth. Limits apply to the theoretical dive depth.

 see the *PADI* Adventures in Diving Manual

2. You

Do you have experience with the conditions? If not, it's better to gain experience with them before making deep dives. Do you have experience with the depth? Try to increase your experience with depth gradually.

How do you feel about the dive? If you feel unduly anxious, perhaps a less stressful dive is in order. How is your health? Factors that can predispose you toward DCS, such as fatigue, suggest a shallow dive well within no stop limits, or perhaps canceling the dive altogether. It's okay for a dive to feeling challenging - that's part of the fun of diving. However, if you start wishing the dive was over before you've even started, listen to your feelings and skip it. Diving is supposed to be enjoyable, not something to endure.

3. Previous dives

Is this a repetitive dive? If so, consult your computer (or RDP) to be sure you have a reasonable allowable bottom time. The general recommendations are to avoid repetitive diving deeper than the previous dive and to avoid repetitive dives deeper than 30 metres/100 feet.

In personalizing your depth limit, be sure to consider previous dives and your allowable no stop time on a repetitive dive.

4. Proximity of emergency care

How far is it to the nearest medical facility in case of an accident? How far to a recompression chamber? The longer it would take to reach these, the shallower and more conservative you'll want to plan your dive.

5. Your buddy

What training and experience does your buddy have? If less than you, plan the dive based on your buddy's training and experience. How does your buddy feel? Consider your buddy's psychological and physical conditions as you would your own.

Equipment for Deep Diving

Established recreational depth limits help determine the performance limits of recreational dive equipment, yet deep diving does have equipment considerations. It's your responsibility to be properly equipped for the demands of the deep diving environment, as well as to observe the limits.

Exercise 2 – What is a Deep Dive?

1. A recreational deep dive is any dive deeper than _____, but no deeper than _____ .
   - ☐ a. 18 metres/60 feet, 30 metres/100 feet
   - ☐ b. 18 metres/60 feet, 40 metres/130 feet
   - ☐ c. 30 metres/100 feet, 40 metres/130 feet

2. Which of the following are reasons why 30 metres/100 feet is recommended as the optimum deep diving depth limit (check all that apply)?
   - ☐ a. deeper dives have less available light
   - ☐ b. deeper dives are shorter
   - ☐ c. deeper dives have less to see
   - ☐ d. deeper dives have increased DCS risk
   - ☐ e. deeper dives have increased likelihood of nitrogen narcosis

3. Which of the following are factors to consider when personalizing your depth limit (check all that apply)?
   - ☐ a. the environment
   - ☐ b. previous dives
   - ☐ c. your physical/mental condition
   - ☐ d. your buddy
   - ☐ e. proximity of emergency care

How'd you do?

1. b. **2.** *a, b, d, e. Not "c" because deep dives may have as much to see as a shallower dive.* **3.** *a, b, c, d, e.*

Study Objectives

Underline/highlight the answers to these questions as you read:

1. How do you determine if your personal equipment is suitable for deep diving?

2. What five specialized pieces of equipment are recommended for deep diving?

3. What makes up a surface support station?

4. What five guidelines should you follow when using a dive computer?

Learn more...

Your Personal Equipment

You'll probably find most of your current dive equipment suitable for deep diving, though you may need to address maintenance, configuration or add components before deep diving with it. Each piece has its considerations.

Learn more *see* The Encyclopedia of Recreational Diving, Dive Equipment, 3rd ed

Regulator

Probably the most important feature to look for in a deep diving regulator is a balanced first stage. A balanced first stage breathes evenly, regardless of cylinder pressure, and delivers adequate air without excessive effort, even during moderate exercise. You may want to consider a high-performance second stage design. These include balanced adjustable second stages, pilot valve second stages and Venturi assisted second stages. Many high-end second stages have more than one of these to enhance performance.

Today, all but the most inexpensive regulators feature balanced first stages and provide sufficient flow for recreational deep diving. The upper line models have the higher performance second stages, which are nice to have for recreational deep diving. If you're considering continuing into the Tec Deep Diver course, you may want to

Probably the most important feature to look for in a deep diving regulator is a balanced first stage.

invest in a high end, top of the line model suited to tec diving now. Note that most tec divers use the threaded DIN first stage connector rather than a yoke system that is popular in most areas.

Maintenance plays a vital part in regulator performance. As you've learned, you should rinse your regulator thoroughly after each dive and have it serviced annually. If you notice any excessive breathing resistance or tendency to free flow, have it checked before using it again, no matter how recently you had it serviced.

Submersible pressure gauge

Whether you use a conventional SPG or an air-integrated dive computer, make sure all parts, including the gauge itself, the swivels, and all connections/transmitters obtain annual service with your regulator. The SPG routes high-pressure air directly from your cylinder, so minor leaks can quickly turn into major leaks. If you note any bubbles coming from the SPG, the hose or a connection, have it checked immediately.

You may suspect that a conventional mechanical SPG is nearing the end of its useful life when it begins to read high. This is because the internal tube that flexes in response to cylinder pressure becomes weak, bending more easily than it should. This gives an inaccurate reading, typically (but not always) accompanied by a not returning all the way to zero when you depressurize the regulator. These indicate that the gauge may fail soon, which usually results in an internal leak and rupture of the gauge blowout plug. If you notice that your pressure always seems high compared to the fill station and/or that the gauge doesn't read zero without pressure, have the gauge checked or replace it.

The Differences Between Balanced and Unbalanced First Stages

Why do balanced first stages make a better choice than unbalanced designs? Because balanced first stages:

- breathe easier at greater depths.
- are more capable of supplying air to accessories such as low pressure BCD and dry suit inflators.
- are better able to supply the needs of two divers in an alternate air source gas sharing emergency.

In addition, changes in cylinder pressure don't affect balanced first stage regulators, so it doesn't become more difficult to breathe as you use up your air.

The accompanying diagrams depict how balanced and unbalanced piston first stages function. In studying these illustrations, notice that:

- In unbalanced first stages, cylinder pressure works to force the piston open. To give the piston sufficient leverage to overcome this force, the valve orifice must be smaller.

Also, as the cylinder pressure diminishes, it's easier for air in the intermediate pressure chamber to close the piston. This makes it increasingly harder to breathe from this first stage as the dive progresses.

- Cylinder pressure doesn't affect the operation of the balanced valve. Pressure exerts around the piston stem, but it is balanced so the force doesn't force the piston into either the open or closed position. Since there's no need to compensate for cylinder pressure affecting piston operation, the orifice can be much larger to provide superior air flow.

A few manufacturers have innovated ways to make what some argue are actually unbalanced first stage designs offer performance comparable to balanced designs. These ways include using oversize pistons or special balance chambers. Without getting into a semantic argument over whether these are "true" balanced first stages, the important thing is that they perform just as well.

Simple unbalanced first stages, such as the one depicted in the example, have largely vanished from the marketplace. Thus, with a few exceptions, you don't need to be overly concerned with getting a regulator with less than desirable performance characteristics.

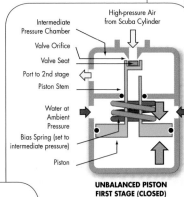

UNBALANCED PISTON FIRST STAGE (CLOSED)

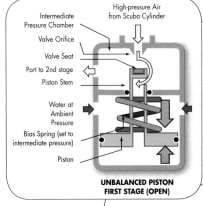

UNBALANCED PISTON FIRST STAGE (OPEN)

BALANCED PISTON FIRST STAGE (CLOSED)

BALANCED PISTON FIRST STAGE (OPEN)

Buoyancy Compensating Device (BCD)

Virtually any state-of-the-art BCD should be suitable for recreational deep diving. Inspect it periodically for possible leaks, and be sure the low-pressure inflator operates properly.

Since you use your air or enriched air faster as you dive deeper, you may want to use a higher capacity cylinder than usual. However, you can deep dive with regular cylinders, though for not as long.

Cylinders

Since you use air or enriched air faster as you dive deeper, it's better to have more than less, even if you consume it slowly compared to other divers. Normally, deep dive with a 12 litre/71.2 cubic foot or larger cylinder. Some high capacity cylinders hold about half again to *twice* as much as a 12 litre/71.2 cubic foot cylinder. No matter what size you use, keep a close eye on both your air supply and your no decompression limit. On some dives, you may run out of allowable no stop time while you still have plenty of air to breathe. This is particularly true when you dive deeper than 30 metres/100 feet. On most deep dives using a computer with a multilevel profile and/or EANx, you will run low on air/EANx first.

Exposure suit

Even at the same dive site, the suit that keeps you comfortable at 12 metres/40 feet may not be adequate for a dive to 36 metres/120 feet, for several reasons:

First, you're more likely to drop through a thermocline into colder water on a deep dive. Wear exposure protection based on the planned depth temperature, not the surface temperature.

Second, a wet suit compresses under pressure, losing its ability to insulate as it does. At 40 metres/130 feet, a wet suit has only about a quarter of its surface insulating ability. If the water's not too cold at depth, or your time at depth is relatively short, you'll usually return to shallow water before you chill. Otherwise, you may want to use a thicker wet suit, or a dry suit with undergarments based on the temperature at depth. You can learn more about dry suit diving in the PADI Dry Suit Diver Specialty course.

A wet suit loses insulation with depth, so in cooler climates, you may want to use a dry suit for deep dives.

Learn more *see the PADI* Dry Suit Diver Manual *and* Dry Suit Diving *video*

Alternate air source

On all dives - but especially deep dives, it's important to ensure that you can find your alternate air source quickly. To do this, secure it in the triangle formed by your chin and the corners of your rib cage (something you've probably already learned). This also prevents it from dragging and filling with sand.

Some divers have their alternate air sources detuned to prevent accidental free flow, but for deep diving this probably isn't the best way to go. At 40 metres/130 feet when you're sharing air, your regulator must deliver *ten times* as much as when you're breathing alone at the surface; detuning only adds to the resistance your buddy will have to cope with amid an emergency.

A better suggestion is to use an *adjustable* second stage or a Venturi assisted model with a dive/predive switch. Adjust the alternate to breathe slightly harder, or leave it on "predive" so it doesn't freeflow easily. During your predive safety check, show your buddy how to readjust it or switch to "dive" in the event it's needed. Note that your buddy can still breathe from the alternate in the predive setting.

To prevent your alternate second stage from freeflowing, adjust it to breathe slightly harder or leave it on the "predive" setting. Be sure to show your buddy how to readjust it and switch to the "dive" setting.

You may want to consider adding a pony bottle to your equipment when you deep dive. A pony bottle is an independent small cylinder, with its own regulator, that provides additional air without buddy assistance. Because the pony bottle is independent and provides additional air, it helps assure that you have ample gas to reach the surface safely in an emergency. Your pony bottle is for emergency only. Don't include its air in planning your dive.

It is important that the regulator used for the pony cylinder is easily identified, and that it cannot be mistaken for the diver's primary regulator. This can be achieved by ensuring the second stage, mouthpiece, or pony cylinder hose are a different color than the diver's primary regulator. You may want to consider a different shape and style of second stage or mouthpiece from that of your primary. Use of a physical item, which covers the mouthpiece and must be physically removed before the regulator can be used, is yet another solution.

Buddy teams should confirm the procedures that will be used, should a diver need to switch to a pony cylinder and end the dive. Have a pony bottle serviced annually, just like your regulator.

You may want to consider adding a pony bottle for deep diving. A pony bottle provides an additional independent air source in an emergency.

Another option that is a spin off from tec diving, cavern diving and recreational penetration diving are H- and Y-valves. These valves allow you to attach two separate regulators to a single cylinder. If one were to fail (and freeflow), you or your buddy would close the portion of the valve supplying that regulator, and you would end the dive using the other. When using this configuration, you normally have your primary second stage and your alternate second stage each on a different first stage. In deep diving, an advantage of this is that when sharing air with a buddy, your buddy's supply feeds through an entirely separate first stage. This may provide better performance in delivering the dense air at depth.

Unlike a pony bottle, H- and Y- valves don't give you any additional gas supply. For this reason, it's common to use them with high capacity cylinders, providing both a redundant breathing source and additional air or enriched air. Some divers also use the TecRec configuration of having a standard length hose on one second stage and a two metre/seven foot hose on the other. The shorter hose second stage hangs on a lanyard around your neck and the longer hose comes straight down along the cylinder, up at the waist, across your chest, behind you neck and into your mouth. In an air-sharing emergency, you give your buddy the second stage from your mouth and switch to the shorter hose second stage. The TecRec configuration isn't mandatory for recreational deep diving, but there's nothing wrong with it and you may prefer it, especially if the Tec Deep Diver certification is one of your goals.

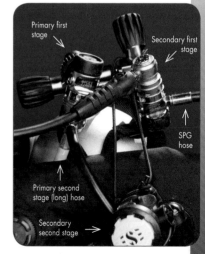

H- and Y-valves provide two separate first and second stages. Some divers like to use the TecRec configuration with H-valves.

Gauges and computers

As in shallow diving, for deep diving you need a way to track depth, time and direction. This means you'll need at least a depth gauge, dive watch/dive timer and compass. Today, most divers use a dive computer, which tracks depth, time and no stop time remaining and (in some models) air supply and estimated air supply time remaining (more about computers later). Many deep divers also have depth gauges with built in timers as a backup to use with dive tables in the remote possibility that their computer fails, or simply two dive computers.

Modern dive computers and other instruments are highly accurate instruments that stand up to a surprising amount of abuse, though you should still treat them with respect. Avoid dropping or banging them, obviously, and don't leave them in direct sunlight for long periods. If you must leave gauges in a sunny area, turn them face down away from the sun, or even better, cover them with a

light color towel or something similar. Modern dive computers work for years with little care beyond rinsing, drying and replacing the batteries as specified by the manufacturer, though it's a good idea to have their accuracy checked periodically.

Today, most divers use dive computers. In deep diving, many divers also wear a backup depth gauge and timer, or a second dive computer.

Do You *Need* a Fresh Water Calibrated Computer When Diving in Fresh Water?

Because salt water exerts more pressure per metre/foot than fresh water, some divers wonder whether you need to reset your dive computer (or depth gauge) from saltwater calibration to freshwater calibration (assuming you can - not all dive computers do this). Similarly, some dive computers and gauges are freshwater calibrated - must you set these for salt water before diving in the ocean? The answer to both is "no." Here's why.

A dive computer (or depth gauge) actually measures *pressure*, which it converts to a depth. So as far as computing your no stop limits, pressure is all that matters.

You use dive tables based on depth, but again, the tables are really calculating *pressures*. When your dive computer reads 30 metres/100 feet, the *pressure* is the same, whether you're in salt water or fresh water. In fresh water, the depth from the surface (if measured with a line) would be 31.4 metres/103 feet, but the *pressure* is still

equal to 30 metres/100 feet of salt water. Since your decompression status is related to pressure, your computer will give you the same no stop limit either way - it's only concerned with the pressure.

If you're using the RDP and a depth gauge, there's still no issue. The RDP is a saltwater calibrated table. If your depth gauge is calibrated for salt water, again, it's only the pressure that matters. If your depth gauge is calibrated for fresh water, the slight difference would cause you (at times) to be more conservative and round up to a higher depth than necessary.

However, note that fresh water dives at *altitude* require depth adjustments due to differences in atmospheric pressure. If your freshwater dives will be at altitude (about 300 metres/1000 feet), see your PADI Instructor or Dive Center about the PADI Altitude Diver course.

Special Deep Diving Equipment

Beyond your personal equipment there are five other pieces of gear that can enhance or affect your deep diving. Not all are absolutely necessary for every deep dive, but each can add to your performance and/or safety.

Reference line

Descents and ascents are easier when you have a reference, and this is particularly true on a deep dive with limited visibility. A reference line is simply that – a rope, usually 13mm/1/2 inch or larger, that you use for controlling descents/ascents, maintaining buddy contact and to simplify safety stops.

Often, your reference line is simply the boat's mooring or anchor line. If the boat is moored or anchored properly with adequate scope, the line is particularly useful in a current because it's usually well secured at the bottom. You can pull yourself along it without worrying about dislodging it, greatly reducing the effort you use to reach the bottom while avoiding being swept down current. Once on the bottom the current's usually much weaker, so you swim into the current during the dive. When you run low on air or no stop time, you return to the line and ascend along it so you don't get swept down current as you come up.

In rough seas, the anchor line jerks up and down in shallow water as the boat rises and falls on the waves, which can make it difficult to use as a reference line. As you go deeper, this is often less of a problem due to the natural stretch of the line and the counterweighing effect of chain near the bottom. If the motion isn't too bad, swim to either side with a hand on the line, letting your arm swing with it like a shock absorber so you're not yanked up and down. In areas where waves are common, some divers carry a jon line – a strong, short cord with a loop at each end that they can snug around the anchor line and hang on to. The cord helps dampen the anchor line's motion.

If you're not diving from a boat, or to have a more direct, vertical descent, you or the crew can suspend a separate weighted reference line from a float or the boat stern. This may be a better choice in locations where the boat moors or anchors away from the desired site, then drifts back so it sits directly over the site. Except when drift diving, it's best not to use a separate float when there's strong current, however, because you're likely to drag the float, line and anchor/weight and end up downstream. As the anchor/weight drags along the bottom, it can cause severe and irreversible damage to the aquatic life. To eliminate that risk, descend/ascend following the mooring or anchor line.

Descents and ascents are easiest with a reference. The boat's mooring or anchor line often makes an excellent reference line for descending and ascending.

Line Divers

What kind of line should you use in the aquatic environment? Rope materials have differing properties, and the same diameter in different materials will have different strength.

Regardless of the type of rope you use, be sure to properly dispose of any unused parts. Synthetic materials stay in the environment for thousands of years and carelessly discarded natural rope can destroy a variety of aquatic organisms. Here are some of the popular types, with characteristics of each.

Synthetic rope - Synthetic materials are nonbiodegradable and very strong for their size, making them overall the best choices for inwater applications. However, knots in synthetic material slip more easily, so proper tying is important. Synthetic is the only choice for permanent moorings and other applications where a rope must remain for a long time. Synthetic also requires less care; you can put it away wet without worrying about it.

Nylon - The strongest rope material, nylon is suited for all-round diving applications. It isn't damaged by most chemicals or marine growth, but it stretches the most, especially three-strand. Nylon is softer than other synthetics, so it's easy to work with when tying or splicing.

Polyester - Polyester isn't as strong as nylon, but it stretches less, which can be advantageous when you need a steady tension. Otherwise, it's very much like nylon.

Polypropylene - Polypropylene is very popular with boaters because it's inexpensive and floats. It's especially suited for swim lines and trail lines, not just because it floats, but because you can buy it in bright colors. However, polypropylene knots don't hold as well as with nylon or polyester, and it's only about half as strong as nylon.

Natural rope - You won't find natural materials commonly in the marine environment because they rot if they're not dried after use, and they swell when wet, causing knots to jam. In cold weather, wet natural rope freezes. They're not as strong as synthetic rope, but they knot and hold well.

Because natural rope biodegrades, such as manila or sisal, it is useful in applications where it may be abandoned in the environment. This includes uses such as a temporary marker buoy that might blow away and sink in an unexpected storm, or for lifting an object that, if it broke free during the lift, would sink someplace beyond retrieval. Natural rope should be uncoiled to dry before storing, inspected frequently and replaced as it breaks down. Even with proper maintenance, natural rope will not last as long as synthetic rope.

Braid or Three Strand - Synthetic or natural rope is either braided or twisted three strand. Braid is sometimes slightly stronger for a given material and thickness, plus it coils more easily and frays more slowly on a cut end. It also costs a bit more. Three strand stretches more, but is much easier to weave and splice. The advantage here is that splices are much stronger than knots for permanent applications, such as joining an anchor chain to a rope, or making permanent loops in dock lines or similar applications.

Strength - When choosing a rope for its working strength, allow an ample extra margin. Remember that a rope weakens with repeated use and abrasion. In addition, a knot reduces a rope's strength by as much as 66 percent by concentrating stress in a single spot. The rule of thumb is that a rope's working strength is one-fifth its breaking strength.

Emergency breathing equipment

Ideally, you'll never need emergency breathing equipment after a deep dive, but like your alternate air source, it's a good idea to have it – just in case. Given the short no stop limits and rapid air consumption of deep dives, it's reassuring to have extra air waiting for a safety or emergency decompression stop.

The simplest emergency breathing equipment is a cylinder and regulator suspended at 5 metres/15 feet, next to the reference line. Some charter dive boats have second stages on long hoses that reach down to 5 metres/15 feet, eliminating the need for a cylinder. Dive boats often suspend a weighted horizontal bar at 5 metres/15 feet, too, so divers can spread out and hang on for their safety stop instead of crowding a single spot on the reference line. These bars may have cylinders/hoses at each end as well.

Whatever type emergency breathing equipment is used, it's a good idea to have enough second stages for all divers to breathe from it at once.

In some situations, it may be impractical to set up emergency breathing equipment for a deep dive. When this is the situation, plan your dive extra conservatively so you have more than ample reserve air. This is a good time to consider diving with a high capacity cylinder with an H- or Y-valve, or a pony bottle.

Ideally, you'll never need emergency breathing equipment after a deep dive – but it's good to have it, just in case.

Extra weight

Your cylinder may lighten as much as two or three kilograms/five or six pounds from full to nearly empty. If this makes you a bit buoyant so you have difficulty maintaining your safety stop, extra weight comes in handy.

You usually leave extra weights clipped to a line or in a mesh bag (typically with the emergency cylinder). These may be loose weights that you drop in your BCD pocket, or weights with snap hooks to clip to a D ring on your weight belt or BCD.

Dive light

Water absorbs light, so even in clear water a dive light comes in handy for bringing out vivid colors or peering into cracks and holes. In lower visibility environments it may be significantly darker at depth, so a light helps with reading gauges and keeping track of your buddy. A compact light, such a night diving backup light, may be all you need, though you'll want a full-sized, primary light for sites that are very dark at depth.

First aid and emergency oxygen

It's recommended that you have first aid and emergency oxygen at hand whenever you're diving, not just deep diving. Your instructor will review DCS and oxygen first aid as part of your PADI Deep Diver course; you can learn more about handling emergencies in the PADI Rescue Diver course, and the Emergency First Response program.

Learn more *see the PADI* Rescue Diver Manual and Rescue Diver Video

Surface Support Stations

For convenience, you can suspend your reference line, emergency breathing equipment and extra weights from a float or even a small boat, forming a *surface support station*. You can tow the station during your dive, or leave it in place with a small anchor. Besides carrying deep diving equipment, you can equip a surface support station with a dive flag to warn off boaters.

You use a surface support station mainly when diving from shore. However, if you're diving from a boat and have some doubt whether you'll be able to relocate it when you surface, you may opt to tow a surface support station. If you elect to do so, use caution and don't attempt to go too far. The station will have considerable drag, raising your air consumption and workload, especially if you have to pull it against a current or wind.

Using Dive Computers

The modern dive computer has become a standard piece of equipment among most recreational divers, and is the mainstay in most (but not all) tec diving. Given the ease they provide in planning and controlling your dive, plus the added dive time you enjoy with EANx and/or a multilevel profile, this comes as no surprise.

While dive computers changed diving and brought new advantages compared to the old days of diving with tables like the Recreational Dive Planner (still the favorite standby in case you have a computer problem), like all dive gear, computers require proper use. They don't grant you complete freedom to disregard the basic principles you learned regarding decompression theory in your PADI Open Water Diver course.

Always read and follow the manufacturer's instructions. The following guidelines apply specifically to dive computers:

1. Always use your dive computer as a no stop (no decompression) device. Stay well within its limits and ascend to shallower depths before you run out of time at your present depth. Most computers handle decompression stops, but that takes you into the realm of tec diving for a whole host of reasons.

2. Don't share computers. Every diver needs a personal one. Computers track profiles very closely and it's unlikely that you and your buddy will have identical profiles. Because computers track nitrogen release during surface intervals, you don't swap computers between dives. Your computer is yours for the entire diving day, or even longer if it hasn't cleared before resuming diving the next day. If your buddy doesn't have a computer, then your buddy must dive within RDP limits.

3. Follow the more conservative computer, yours, your buddy's or your back up if you use one. Differences may reflect the variances between your profiles, or differences in the way various computer types calculate. If your buddy uses dive tables, this also means your dive ends, too, at the table limit.

4. If your computer malfunctions during a dive, make a normal ascent and a safety stop (air permitting). Follow the manufacturer's instructions regarding resuming diving, which may require you to wait 12 or more hours. You may be able to resume diving with the RDP if your depths, times and surface intervals fall within its limits. Unfortunately, multilevel computer dives don't always fall within table limits (tables assume you spend the entire dive at the deepest depth), so this may not work out.

5. Don't follow your computer blindly. Compare yours with your buddy's – if you've been on the same dive profiles, there shouldn't be huge discrepancies (but some discrepancy is normal). Fortunately, a malfunctioning computer rarely gives erroneous data. More typically, it conks out completely or displays garbage. In any case, carry the RDP in case your computer fails, or better yet, a backup computer – especially when deep diving.

Don't follow your computer blindly. Compare yours with your buddy's and pay attention to huge discrepancies.

Computer Misconceptions

Computers revolutionized the way we dive, giving us more allowable no stop time on multilevel profiles, and less error potential because they track depth and time for us. No one would want to go back to diving without them, but there are a few misconceptions to be aware of.

Misconception - Computers track something in your body. No, computers are simply calculators that read the depth, time and apply them to a mathematical model (a.k.a *algorithm*). There's no physical link between the computer and your internal physiology. The computer simply assumes that you have it with you at all times while diving (so be sure you do).

Misconception - Computers are more reliable than tables. Both computers and dive tables are based on the same types of underlying models and theoretical basis, so they're comparably reliable. Computers custom calculate no stop limits based on your actual dive profile, so they're better able to adapt the model to your actual dive, so they're more flexible than dive tables - not more reliable.

Misconception - A computer that costs more is safer than a cheaper one. Fortunately, what you invest in a dive computer relates to features, not the ability to apply a decompression model reliably. Even the less costly models can be expected to do that, but investing more gives you a lot of desirable extra features.

Misconception - The computer says it, so I can do it. The same guidelines apply to diving with computers and dive tables: Make dives successively shallower; avoid up-and-down "sawtooth" profiles; make safety stops, don't make repetitive dives deeper than 30 metres/100 feet, don't push each level of multilevel dives up to its maximum limit; avoid "bounce" diving, etc. Breaking these rules may increase your risk of decompression sickness whether you're using a table or a computer. The computer still gives you the numbers if you break these guidelines, not because it's okay, but so you won't be stuck without any information at all.

To learn more about dive computers, decompression theory and multilevel diving, ask your PADI Instructor or PADI Dive Center about the PADI Multilevel Diver Specialty course. This course teaches you about dive computers and their applications in multilevel diving. In addition, check out the decompression models section in Chapter Five, the Physiology of Diving in *The Encyclopedia of Recreational Diving, Third Edition* available at your PADI Resort or Dive Center.

Exercise 3 – Equipment for Deep Diving

1. One consideration in your personal equipment for deep diving is locating the alternate air source in the triangle between your chin and the corners of your rib cage.
   ☐ True   ☐ False

2. Specialized equipment for deep diving includes (check all that apply):

   ☐ a. emergency breathing equipment.
   ☐ b. dive computers.
   ☐ c. extra weights.

3. A surface support station consists of (check all that apply):
   ☐ a. reference line.
   ☐ b. emergency breathing equipment.
   ☐ c. weights.
   ☐ d. an underwater light.

4. Divers should not share dive computers.
   ☐ True   ☐ False

How'd you do?
1. True. *2.* a, c. Not "b" because computers can be used on all dives. *3.* a, b, c. *4.* True.

Deep Diving Techniques: Buddy Contact and Neutral Buoyancy

Study Objectives

Underline/highlight the answers to these questions as you read:

1. What are two techniques for maintaining buddy contact during deep dives?

2. How should you maintain neutral buoyancy on a deep dive?

Like any specialty activity, deep diving has unique techniques, procedures and recommendations. Most of these simply extend or adapt the diving procedures you already know to diving below 18 metres/60 feet.

Maintaining Buddy Contact

As you're aware, you should stay with your buddy on any dive, but on a deep dive, it's extra important. If you and your buddy lose track of each other on a shallow dive you can usually surface, regroup and continue the dive. On a deep dive, you seldom have sufficient air and no stop time to continue the dive, so having to surface usually means the dive's over. In addition, if your computer has a problem, although you may carry a second timepiece and depth gauge, you may need to rely on your buddy's for backup.

Stay closer to your buddy than you might on a shallower dive. During descents and ascents, make eye contact

frequently and try to stay at about the same level (more about descents and ascents in the next section). Following a reference line will help you stay together because if you are slightly separated, you only have to look up or down the

line to regroup. If you reach the bottom slightly ahead of your buddy, stay where you are until your buddy catches up.

Stay closer to your buddy on a deep dive than you might on a shallower dive.

When you reach your planned depth, stay near each other. You can maintain eye contact and signal easier by swimming side-by-side. Try to stay within touching distance, even if the visibility is good. If visibility is poor, you may want to hold hands, wrists or lightly hold a short piece of rope looped at both ends, to stay together.

Neutral Buoyancy for Deep Dives

As you've already experienced on shallow dives, your buoyancy changes as you descend and ascend due primarily to the compression of your exposure suit. The air you add to your BCD to offset the loss of buoyancy also compresses and expands as you descend and ascend. Deep dives magnify these changes because the pressure change is greater. This means you need to monitor and adjust your buoyancy closely as you go down and when you come up. However, you'll notice that as you get deeper, the amount of buoyancy change per metre/per foot of depth is less than when you're shallower. This is because the proportional change is less the deeper you are.

Begin the dive properly weighted. Start by doing a buoyancy check if necessary. As you recall, while fully equipped, you should float at eye level with an empty BCD while holding a normal breath. When you exhale, you should sink. For deep dives, it's ideal to check your weighting with a nearly empty cylinder. This is because your scuba cylinder can be two kilograms/five pounds (or more) lighter when it's nearly empty at the end of a dive. The extra buoyancy could make you struggle to stay at the safety stop. If you check your buoyancy with a full cylinder, after you're properly weighted add about two kilograms/five pounds to compensate for the air you'll use during the dive.

If you check your buoyancy with a full cylinder, after you're properly weighted add about two kilograms/ five pounds to compensate for the air you'll use during the dive.

As you descend and the pressure compresses your exposure suit, add air to your BCD periodically (and to your dry suit if you're diving in one) so that you reach the bottom neutrally buoyant. Don't wait until you get there to adjust because you'll likely be very negatively buoyant and hit the bottom. Depending upon how much

exposure protection you're wearing, you may need a moderate amount of air to achieve neutral buoyancy – more than you're used to on shallower dives.

 When using a dry suit, it's very important to add air to your suit frequently as you descend. You need to do this not just to maintain neutral buoyancy, but to equalize the suit and prevent a dry suit squeeze. **Failure to equalize a dry suit can cause a painful squeeze and possible injury**. As mentioned earlier, it's a good idea to complete the PADI Dry Suit Diver Specialty course if you'll be diving in a dry suit.

It's perhaps more important to maintain neutral buoyancy as you ascend. Remember that all the air you put in your BCD and dry suit expands as you ascend, so you need to vent air from them frequently. The idea is to maintain a proper ascent rate and arrive at your safety stop neutrally buoyant (more about ascents later). If you find yourself a bit buoyant at the safety stop despite your predive weight check, you can clip on a weight left with the emergency breathing equipment.

Exercise 4 – Deep Diving Techniques: Buddy Contact and Neutral Buoyancy

1. To maintain buddy contact, you should
   - ☐ a. swim side-by-side at your planned depth.
   - ☐ b. avoid using a reference line.

2. To help you sink faster during deep diving descents, don't adjust your buoyancy until you reach the bottom.
   ☐ True   ☐ False

How'd you do?
1. a. 2. False. Adjust your buoyancy as you go so you reach the bottom neutrally buoyant. If wearing a dry suit, you also need to add air to the suit to prevent suit squeeze.

Deep Diving Techniques: Descents and Ascents

you may prefer to swim or pull yourself along in a more horizontal attitude. You can still make a head-up descent by keeping yourself angled so your body and legs remain somewhat below head level.

If you descend vertically feet-first, be cautious as you near the bottom that you don't kick up silt or damage any aquatic organisms with your fins.

Study Objectives

Underline/highlight the answers to these questions as you read:

1. How do you make a head-up descent, and why is this important in deep diving?

2. What are two techniques for slowing or stopping descents/ascents along a reference line with your hands occupied?

3. What are four steps to follow while descending/ascending without a reference?

4. What are two techniques for estimating an 18 metre/60 foot per minute or slower ascent rate?

A head-up descent, in which your head remains higher than your feet and body, reduces disorientation due to vertigo. If you descend vertically, be cautious not to kick up the bottom or damage aquatic organisms as you near the bottom.

Head-up Descents

Descending into either deep or shallow water, you want to maintain your orientation and sense of direction. A head-up descent in which your head remains higher than your feet reduces disorientation due to vertigo. It also makes it easier to equalize your ears and control your buoyancy as you descend.

Descending feet first vertically is the most straightforward head-up position, and probably what you would do along a nearly vertical line or other reference. However, without a reference or following an angled anchor line,

Controlling Descents and Ascents

It's important to prevent rapid descents and ascents. A rapid descent may result in an ear, sinus, mask or dry suit squeeze if you can't equalize fast enough. As mentioned before, a rapid ascent can cause you to miss your safety stop, and very rapid ascents can lead to decompression sickness or lung overexpansion injuries.

The surest way to control descents and ascents, in addition to controlling your buoyancy, is to descend and ascend along an anchored or weighted reference line. Descend/ascend with one hand on the line, while using the other to equalize and control your BCD. Grasp the line if you begin to sink/rise too rapidly, and adjust your BCD. The reference line shouldn't replace proper buoyancy control, but rather provide another way to assure a controlled descent/ascent rate.

If your hands are occupied (e.g., you're carrying a camera and equalizing your ears), you can still slow or stop your descent on a line by locking your elbow around it. To remain stopped for a while with both hands free, wrap your leg around the line. These techniques are especially useful when diving in a moderate current so you aren't carried away from the boat.

You can slow or stop a descent with occupied hands by locking your elbow on a reference line.

To free your hands while holding your depth, wrap your leg around the reference line.

When you don't have a reference line, a sloping bottom or wall works well as a reference. You want to avoid grabbing a wall, for example, if it's teeming with fragile organisms, but a visual reference aids controlling your descent significantly. Watch the wall or sloping bottom, so you'll be able to see your speed increase and decrease, cuing you to adjust your buoyancy.

A slopping bottom or wall provides a visual reference you can use to gauge your descent/ascent rate.

In some instances, you may have to descend or ascend without any reference. While this isn't ideal and can be disorienting, four steps make reference-less descents/ascents something you can do without too much difficulty: First, maintain a head-up position so you don't become disoriented. Second, make frequent eye contact with your buddy and stay close together. Third, watch the depth on your dive computer and adjust your buoyancy so you don't exceed your maximum depth while descending or 18 metres/60 feet per minute or the rate specified by your computer (whichever is slower) while ascending. Fourth, on ascents make a three minute (or longer) safety stop at 5 metres/15 feet and listen for boats. Wait for any noise to pass before continuing your ascent. After the stop, come to the surface with one hand over your head. Look up for obstructions and surface carefully.

Estimating Ascent Rates

As any diver knows, a proper ascent rate is important in avoiding decompression illness. Whether you ascend with or without a reference, it's important that you monitor and maintain a rate not greater than 18 metres/60 feet metres per minute, or even slower with most dive computers.

The easier way to track your ascent rate is to use your dive computer. Most computers have ascent rate alarms (visual and/or audible) that alert you if you exceed their maximum rate. Some have "speedometers" that show your ascent speed, making it easy to tell when you're speeding up or slowing down. Either way, vent air from your BCD and dry suit (if you're wearing one) or otherwise slow your ascent based on what your computer tells you.

When monitoring your ascent rate, don't neglect to look up. You can ascend looking up, one hand over your head with your BCD hose, and glance at your computer periodically. Some divers hold their computer up, overhead so they can see it and the surface at the same time.

Ascent Rate Mythology

Over the years, diving folklore has drummed up some interesting "facts" about ascent rates. These range from ideas that once had some validity, but have passed their time, to others that have no basis in reality at all.

Myth - The 18 metre/60 foot per minute ascent rate is based on hard data about human physiology. Actually, the rate grew out of a compromise between two groups of U.S. Navy divers.

When the U.S. Navy tables were being revised in the 1950s, the Navy's hardhat divers wanted the ascent rate maintained at 7.6 metres/25 feet per minute, which had been the practice for more than 20 years. A new diver group, however, Navy frogmen, considered that intolerably slow and clamored for 30 metres/100 feet per minute. Those involved in the decision split the difference, and the 18 metre/60 foot per minute rate was born. All U.S. Navy tests for its tables, and the 1980s DSAT tests for the RDP, were based on this rate. Recently, the U.S. Navy changed the ascent rate to 9 metres/30 feet per minute, but the original tests were still based on 18 metres/60 feet per minute.

Today, most dive computers use a rate of 10 metres/30 feet per minute or slower. Some have rates that change depending upon depth, typically getting even slower as you ascend above 10 metres/30 feet. There's nothing wrong with this slower rate, though the majority of testing is actually based on a less conservative rate.

Myth - To ascend at a proper rate, ascend no faster than your smallest bubbles. This guideline may have had some merit in the days before better methods of tracking your ascent, but it's no match for today's dive computers for controlling your ascent. There are several problems with "following your smallest bubbles."

First, exactly what qualifies as a smallest bubble? The smallest you can see, which barely ascends at all, or something larger? If larger, how much? Second, even if you figure that out, you have to keep switching bubbles because bubbles expand and accelerate during ascent. Third, if you're ascending along an anchor line in a current, you don't have bubbles to follow - they're all being whisked downstream.

The flip side is that following your smallest bubbles gives you an option if for some reason you lack any other way to monitor your ascent. And, while a properly equipped diver today has more accurate ways to track ascent rate, watching your small bubbles provides a secondary reference that helps, somewhat, when you're multitasking and can't glance at your computer at the moment. It shouldn't be the *primary* way you monitor your ascent rate, but it can be useful even though it is not precise.

Myth - A slow ascent rate replaces a safety stop. While there's probably some ascent rate slow enough to replace a three minute stop at 5 metres/15 feet, such a rate is probably so slow you'd have difficulty maintaining it. You need to ascend no faster than 18 metres/60 feet per minute (or slower if required by your computer) and make a safety stop.

Myth - You can ascend too slowly. It's true there's a theoretical ascent rate that's "too slow," but on a no stop recreational dive, such a rate is so slow that you probably wouldn't consider yourself to be ascending. Furthermore, your dive computer calculates changes in nitrogen absorption, so it accommodates a slower rate by reducing your no stop time remaining.

Ascending too slow is only a concern on a decompression dive, as in tec diving, but even here it's only a big issue if you're using tables instead of a dive computer. Ascending slower than specified by your computer will make the decompression a bit longer, but again your computer calculates it. Being very precise on your ascent rate - not too slow as well as not too fast - is really only an issue when making a decompression dive (outside of recreational diving anyway) without a dive computer.

That a slower ascent rate isn't much of an issue is highlighted by the 1993 revision of the U.S. Navy ascent rate. Cutting the rate in half from 18 metres/60 feet per minute to 9 metres/30 feet per minute didn't require revising the no stops limits.

If you have a computer problem (very rare, but it can happen), you still need to ascend at an appropriate rate. The easiest way to do this is to stay with your buddy, who likely still has a working computer. If that's not possible and you have a backup depth gauge and watch, you can estimate your rate by comparing your depth with time. It should take about 20 seconds to rise six metres, or 10 seconds to rise 10 feet. Of course, this is the maximum rate; a slower rate is acceptable.

Exercise 5 – Deep Diving Techniques: Descents and Ascents

1. A head-up descent

   ☐ a. helps maintain your orientation.

   ☐ b. should be avoided.

2. If you need to stop on a reference line with both hands free, you should (check all that apply):

   ☐ a. tie yourself to the line with a short cord.

   ☐ b. wrap your leg around the line.

   ☐ c. lock your elbow on the line.

   ☐ d. snap your weight belt around the line.

3. The steps for descents/ascents without a reference include (check all that apply):

   ☐ a. maintaining a head-up position.

   ☐ b. staying close to your buddy.

   ☐ c. monitoring your ascent/descent rate.

   ☐ d. making a safety stop at 5 metres/15 feet on ascents.

4. One way to estimate a proper ascent is

   ☐ a. to watch the bottom fall away as you rise.

   ☐ b. to monitor the ascent indicator on a dive computer.

How'd you do?

1. a. *2.* b, c. Not "a" or "d" because you should never attach yourself to the line any way that you cannot immediately let go. *3.* a, b, c, d. *4.* b.

Deep Diving Techniques:
On the Bottom

Deep Diving Breathing Techniques

Since the first time you put a regulator in your mouth and stuck your head underwater, you've been told to breathe slowly and deeply. This is a standard practice on any dive, but it's especially important while deep diving.

Study Objectives

Underline/highlight the answers to these questions as you read:

1. How should you breathe while deep diving?

2. How do you avoid low air or out-of-air situations on a deep dive?

3. What is the best way to swim without stirring up the bottom, and why is it important?

The reason is that strenuous exercise, fighting a current or anything else that raises your breathing rate can make you demand more air. While modern scuba regulators offer incredible performance, the fact is that the deeper you dive, the denser the air you're breathing, and that will reduce performance compared to a shallower dive. If your breathing demand is high, it's possible to demand more air than even with a properly maintained, balanced regulator can deliver.

Density is only part of the issue. A gas flows less smoothly as the flow speed rises. This happens because as air flows through dive equipment, your trachea and bronchi (windpipe and its branches) and into your lungs, drag from contact with the passage surfaces causes the air to become turbulent. The denser the air, the slower the speed at which this happens. Turbulence disrupts even airflow and increases breathing resistance, which in turn demands

more effort. More effort demands more air, so if you're not careful, you end up breathing harder because you're breathing harder. Breathing slowly and deeply keeps you out of this cycle.

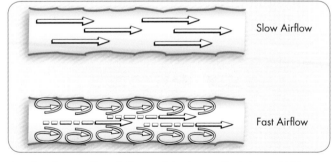

Slow Airflow

Fast Airflow

A gas flows less smoothly as the flow speed rises because of turbulence, which in turn raises breathing resistance.

Another consideration is *dead air space*, which is the portion of each breath that never reaches your lungs.

This consists of your regulator, mouth, trachea and bronchi. After exhaling, the *dead air space* is filled with air high in carbon dioxide; when you inhale, this is the first part of each breath. By breathing deeply, you dilute the dead air with proportionately more fresh air from your scuba cylinder. If you breathe shallowly, on the other hand, dead air makes up more of each breath and you can experience a buildup of carbon dioxide. This can cause a headache, and can make you breathe faster and use your air quicker as your body tries to get rid of the carbon dioxide.

By breathing slowly and deeply, you avoid over-breathing your regulator, excessive breathing resistance and dead air problems. Try to breathe from your stomach and diaphragm, so you fill your lungs from the bottom up. Slow, deep breathing maximizes your respiratory efficiency, so you use your air more slowly.

Learn more *see* The Encyclopedia of Recreational Diving, *The Physiology of Diving*

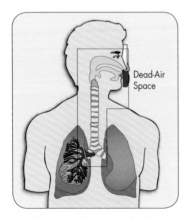

Dead-Air Space

Dead air space is the portion of each breath that doesn't reach your lungs.

If you begin to breathe hard or feel out of breath, slow or stop your activity and catch your breath. Stay relaxed on a deep dive. Establish neutral buoyancy, and move slowly and deliberately. Try to do everything with the least effort possible. Don't try to go as far as you would on shallower dives. You'll find that these steps not only make deep diving more enjoyable and productive, but that they make your air supply last longer, too.

Air Supply Control

Until you experience it, it's difficult to imagine just how much more quickly you use air on a deep dive compared to a shallower dive. Even though the laws of physics dictate that you use air about twice as fast at 30 metres/100 feet as at 10 metres/33 feet, during the dive it seems to go faster than that. One moment you've got a nearly full cylinder, and the next it's time to start up. This highlights an important habit to establish: **To prevent low air or out-of-air emergencies, check your submersible pressure gauge (and other instruments) *frequently.***

You can't check you air supply often enough. The most common preventable cause of deep diving incidents is running very low or out of air - yet it's avoidable if you watch your air supply closely and frequently. Your breathing rate can change quickly, so no one but you can be responsible for closely monitoring your pressure gauge so you reach your ascent point with sufficient air to make a safe ascent, a three-minute safety stop and reach the surface with an appropriate reserve. As you use your gas supply, alert your buddy (and/or divemaster if diving in a group) with ample time to return to your ascent point.

By calculating your air consumption, you can estimate about how long your air will last at a given depth. This aids dive planning, though it's not as useful when you make a deep multilevel dive and don't have a clear idea of how long you'll be spending at each level.

Air integrated dive computers provide a technological solution to estimating air consumption. These computers track your breathing and estimate how much longer your air will last, constantly revising the estimate based on changes in depth or breathing. Usually, these dive computers show you either your no stop time remaining or your estimated air time remaining, whichever is shorter.

Estimating Air Consumption

To use the chart, estimate the depth of your dive and find the column best representing your cylinder size. The approximate total time (in minutes) you'll have underwater is listed on the chart. For example, a dive to 21 metres/70 feet, with a 12 litre/80 cubic foot cylinder will allow you approximately 34 total minutes underwater.

Keep in mind, however, that knowing an estimate of how long a cylinder may last at a certain depth is no substitute for constant monitoring your submersible pressure gauge. Gas supply duration decreases as depth and activity increase, and also based on individual characteristics - a larger person will typically consume more air than a smaller person. The chart's estimated times only apply to a constant depth and activity level. Fitness, stress, experience level, mechanical air losses and water temperature also affect air consumption.

Cylinder Size -- (Litres/Cubic Feet)

Metres/Feet	8/65	10/71	12/80	15/90
18/60	31	34	38	43
20/65	29	32	36	40
21/70	28	30	34	38
23/75	26	29	33	37
24/80	25	28	31	35
26/85	24	26	30	34
27/90	23	25	29	32
29/95	22	24	28	31
30/100	22	23	26	30
34/110	20	22	25	28
37/120	19	20	23	26
40/130	18	19	22	24

Approximate Total time in Minutes
until cylinder is empty. Chart is based on light to moderate diver activity level.

Air Consumption Calculation

How can you tell how long your cylinder will last at a given depth if you've never been that deep before? By using some simple mathematics. All you need is your air consumption rate at a shallower depth, the charts below and a sharp pencil or calculator.

Start by obtaining a record of your air consumption from your dive log. The more dives you work with, the more accurate your calculations will be. Also, dives made primarily at a single level will be more useful than multilevel dives. For each dive, record how many bar/psi you use, the actual dive time and the depth.

Metric

DEPTH Metres	CONVERSION FACTORS Pressure at depth (bar)
0	1.0
3	1.3
6	1.6
9	1.9
12	2.2
15	2.5
18	2.8
21	3.1
24	3.4
27	3.7
30	4.0
33	4.3
36	4.6
39	4.9

1. Determine your air consumption rate at the surface in litres per minute with this formula:

$$\frac{\text{bar used} \times \text{cylinder volume (litres)}}{\text{actual bottom time} \times \text{pressure at depth (bar)}}$$

Example: A diver using a 10 litre cylinder uses 100 bar on a dive to12 metres for 20 minutes. What is the air consumption rate at the surface?

$$\frac{100 \text{ bar} \times 10 \text{ litres}}{20 \text{ min} \times 2.2 \text{ bar}} = 22.73 \text{ litres/minute surface rate}$$

By recording your liter per minute surface rate over several dives and averaging them, you can determine your normal air consumption rate.

1. Determine your psi per minute surface rate with this formula:

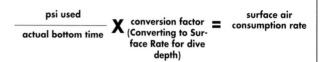

$$\frac{\text{psi used}}{\text{actual bottom time}} \times \text{conversion factor (Converting to Surface Rate for dive depth)} = \text{surface air consumption rate}$$

For example, on a 40 foot dive for 20 minutes in which the diver uses 1500 psi:1500 psi used divided by a 20 minute bottom time x .45 = 33.7 psi per minute surface rate.

By recording your psi per minute surface rate over several dives and averaging them, you can determine your normal air consumption rate. *Note: Make all your calculations with the same type cylinder. If you use different size and/or pressure rated cylinders, you must determine your air consumption for each independently.*

2. To convert your surface rate to your planned depth rate, multiply your surface rate by the *Converting From Surface Rate* conversion factor for the planned depth.

Based on the previous example, if you plan to dive to 100 feet, you can expect your air consumption to be about 136 psi per minute 33.7 x 4.03 = 135.8). If your cylinder is filled to 3000 psi, you could expect it to last about 22 minutes (before allowing for your reserve).

When calculating air supply, keep in mind that excitement, activity and cold all increase your breathing rate, so allow room for error in your dive planning, and always watch your SPG closely. With experience, you'll become proficient at predicting how long a cylinder will last you at a given depth.

2. To determine your air consumption at your planned depth based on your surface rate, multiply your surface rate by the pressure (in bar) for your planned depth, and then divide the air available by that.

Example: Suppose the diver from the previous example plans to dive 30 metres. Approximately how long would you expect a 10 liter cylinder filled to 200 bar to last (before allowing for your reserve)?

Air available = 10 litres x 200 bar = 2000 litres

Air use at 30 metres = 22.73 l/min x 4.0 bar = 90.92 l/min

2000 litres ÷ 90.92 l/min = 22 minutes

Therefore, you would expect the cylinder to last 22 minutes before allowing for your reserve. To account for your reserve pressure, simply subtract it from your starting pressure. In this example, air available would then be 10 litres x 160 bar = 1600 litres; 1600 litres ÷ 90.92 l/m = 17.6 minutes.

Imperial

DEPTH	CONVERSION FACTORS	
Feet	Converting from Surface Rate	Converting to Surface Rate
0	1.00	1.00
10	1.30	0.76
20	1.60	0.62
30	1.91	0.52
40	2.21	0.45
50	2.52	0.40
60	2.82	0.35
70	3.12	0.32
80	3.42	0.29
90	3.73	0.27
100	4.03	0.25
110	4.33	0.23
120	4.64	0.21
130	4.94	0.20

How Much Reserve?

Part of a regular dive plan calls for establishing an appropriate reserve, but what is "appropriate?" Most submersible pressure gauges note a red reserve zone of approximately 50 bar/500 psi, but some dives may call for more reserve. It helps to begin by defining "reserve."

Reserve is the amount of air that you plan to have when you get back on the boat or to shore. Ideally, you should complete your dive, ascent, safety stop and exit procedures without using your reserve air. The reserve is for the unexpected - if you plan to use it, it's not really a reserve.

Since you keep a reserve to help handle unforeseen circumstances, the more complex the dive, the more reserve you want to allow. How much more varies and depends on your judgment, but each of these variables calls for allowing a bit more reserve.

- current
- increased depth
- anything that can delay locating the ascent/exit point
- low visibility
- any exertion that could increase air consumption, including carrying a camera or towing a surface support station
- nearing the no stop limits
- exits in rough seas or through surf

For deep diving, a good all-round air management plan is the rule of thirds used in tec diving - use one-third your air for descent and swimming away from the boat/shore and one-third to return to your safety stop. Keep one-third reserve. Use good judgment, and if in doubt, overestimate rather than underestimate your reserve. For example, if you go *with* the current for the first part of the dive (not generally recommended) you'll use much more air to return, and you should plan accordingly. If you reach your ascent point with more air than you expected, you can use the air in the immediate vicinity before ascending.

Safety stops and reserves - Whatever reserve you select based on dive logistics, ideally plan your dive to include a safety stop without using your reserve. However, if you reach your safety stop with only your reserve left, *use the reserve to make the safety stop.* An exception might be if you have unusual exit conditions that require breathing from your regulator (like an exit through surf), but otherwise, it doesn't make much sense to skip the stop and surface with enough air to have made it. However, if you used your reserve to make the safety stop, then next time you need to plan to turn the dive and head up sooner.

When You Reach the Bottom

As mentioned, you want to reach the bottom neutrally buoyant. Since you don't have time to go far on a deep dive, it's especially important to avoid stirring up the bottom and reducing the visibility. Likewise, you don't want to harm any fragile organisms. Especially if you're descending feet first, switch to a horizontal swimming position while you're still a few metres/feet off the bottom. If you've controlled your buoyancy during your descent, you shouldn't need to kick to stay off the bottom. When other divers are following you down a reference line, get clear of the line when you near the bottom. If you need to make contact with the bottom, find a clear area (no potential hazards or fragile organisms) and settle down gently on your knees. When you leave, use buoyancy control to rise slowly off the bottom, then establish neutral buoyancy and begin swimming. Again, try to avoid kicking up the silt.

If you must make contact with the bottom, find an area clear of sensitive aquatic life and settle gently on your knees.

Exercise 6 – Deep Diving Techniques: On the Bottom

1. The best way to breathe on a deep dive is

    ☐ a. the same as you normally breathe.
    ☐ b. slowly and deeply.

2. The most important step in avoiding low air/out-of-air situations is

    ☐ a. checking your SPG frequently.
    ☐ b. performing air consumption calculations.

3. It's important not to stir up the bottom because
    ☐ a. it causes significant damage to your fins.
    ☐ b. it reduces visibility and can damage aquatic life.

How'd you do?
1. b. *2.* a. *3.* b.

Deep Diving Techniques:
Safety Stops and Emergency Decompression

Up to this point, you've seen numerous references to safety stops, and you're probably well aware that a safety stop is recommended on all dives. A safety stop increases your safety margin by giving your body a chance to release excess dissolved nitrogen before surfacing. It also helps you affirm proper buoyancy control and a proper rate by forcing you to stop before ascending the final 5 metres/15 feet to the surface. This may help reduce the risk of lung overexpansion injuries.

Empirical data, as well as decompression model analyses, support the effectiveness of safety stops. Some limited manned safety stop experiments at the University of Southern California Hyperbaric Chamber showed that safety stops reduced detectable bubble formation in test divers by a factor of five. Analysis of decompression models shows that even cutting your ascent rate in half has less effect on theoretical nitrogen levels than a three-minute stop at 5 metres/15 feet.

It's interesting to note that originally, safety stops were made at 3 metres/10 feet (following U.S. Navy decompression stop guidelines). Later, it became 5 metres/15 feet for several reasons: It's shallow enough to allow good nitrogen release, but it's easier to maintain this depth than 3 metres/10 feet, especially in waves or surge. You have a greater margin for error in maintaining your stop depth at 5 metres/15 feet, and particularly in high traffic areas, it's reassuring to have extra depth when boats pass by.

As you recall from your Open Water Diver course, a safety stop is simply a stop for three to five minutes (or longer if you want) in the 6 metre/20 foot to 3 metre/10 foot range, usually at 5 metres/15 feet. Using the RDP, you don't need to include your safety stop in your bottom time, though you may if you wish for added conservatism. Computers include the stop in their calculations automatically. While you want to stay close to 5 metres/15 feet, don't worry about minor variations - within a metre/a couple feet is fine.

Although it's a stop, you don't have to just sit there and do nothing. If there's nothing interesting to look at, you can put the time to good use by readjusting equipment as needed for a smooth exit, by watching/listening for boats or other overhead obstructions for safety. Some divers like to use the time to practice alternate air source air sharing or other safety drills that they can practice while staying at stop depth.

You can put the time at a safety stop to good use by readjusting equipment as needed for a smooth exit, by watching for hazards or by practicing safety drills.

Besides creating an extra safety margin, safety stops help you avoid the serious situation of accidentally missing an emergency decompression stop. During your safety stop, make a habit of double-checking your no decompression status on your computer or the RDP limits. If you find you've exceeded the no stop limits, extend your stop time cover your emergency decompression requirement.

Recall that when using the Recreational Dive Planner, a safety stop is required if you:

- dive to 30 metres/100 feet or deeper
- end the dive in a pressure group within three pressure groups of the no decompression limit
- reach any limit on the RDP.

Similarly, when diving with a computer you may want to consider a safety stop required if you dive to 30 metres/100 feet or deeper, on any repetitive dive, and on any multilevel dive in which you near a no decompression limit at any depth.

Maintaining Stop Depth with a Reference Line

Unquestionably, apart from ascending along a sloping bottom, the easiest way to make a stop is with a reference line and/or decompression bar. Ascend along the line, adjusting your BCD to maintain neutral buoyancy, until you reach 5 metres/15 feet at chest level. Hold the line so your chest stays about this level, but as mentioned, don't worry about minor variations. If you're on a rising and falling anchor line, holding on to a jon line as described earlier will smooth out the stop a little, but you must be sure to maintain neutral buoyancy.

Most divers seem to prefer a near vertical position during a stop, though a horizontal position is theoretically optimal. However, practically speaking, any position that's comfortable is fine. Just try to keep your chest near the 5 metre/15 foot level.

In clear, currentless water, you may prefer to hover near the line, without actually hanging on to it. You can use the line as a visual reference to maintain your depth. One advantage of this is that several divers don't end up crowding the same point on the line.

In clear, currentless water, you may prefer to hover near your reference line rather than hang onto it. This is especially useful to avoid crowding the line when there are several people diving together.

Stop Depth without a Reference Line

Without a reference line and without a sloping bottom, you'll need to make a midwater stop. You may need to do this while drift diving, or to avoid strong currents near a wall, for example. This requires more effort than a stop with a line, and works best if you coordinate your stop with your buddy.

Ascend slowly to 5 metres/15 feet, adjusting your buoyancy to remain neutral at that depth. Again, try to keep your chest at that level. Since you don't have a reference, use your computer to constantly monitor depth. You can simplify the stop by maintaining your depth by watching your computer with a hand on your buddy, who keeps an eye on the boat, navigation or double checks the RDP if making a tables-based dive. You may want to deploy a Delayed Surface Marker Buoy (DSMB), one with a line long enough for your safety stop depth, to make you location visible to others.

When making a midwater stop, again, maintain a comfortable body position. If there's a slight current, you'll probably find a somewhat horizontal position best so you can swim slowly against it (but avoid overexertion) and not end up down current when you surface.

What is a Delayed Surface Marker Buoy?

A Delayed Surface Marker Buoy (DSMB) is a long sausage-like marker buoy, with an opening at one end. Divers carry it deflated and rolled up in a pocket, or rolled and attached to their reels. At the end of the dive, prior to ascending, a diver can use their alternate air source or exhaled bubbles to inflate the DSMB and send it to the surface, paying out line from their reel as it goes. Divers can then slowly reel the line in as they ascend.

DSMBs provide divers with a visual reference as they ascend and during their safety stops. They are helpful when divers are in a current, or unable to return to the boat for any reason. They also allow boat traffic to identify divers as they begin their ascent.

You can simplify the stop by maintaining your depth by watching your computer with a hand on your buddy, who keeps an eye on the boat, navigation or double checks the RDP if making a tables-based dive.

Emergency Decompression

If you accidentally exceed no stops limits, you'll need to make an emergency decompression stop. Using a computer, follow the procedures dictated by the computer. Typically, your computer will tell you how long to stop at 3 metres/10 feet before you can surface. It's acceptable to make your decompression stop at 5 metres/15 feet, though it will take longer for your computer to clear than it says because you're deeper than 3 metres/10 feet.

If you're using the RDP, these are the rules if you accidentally exceed the no stop limits:

- If you exceed the no decompression limit by no more than five minutes, make an eight minute stop at 5 metres/15 feet. Do not dive again for at least six hours.

- If you exceed the no decompression limit by more than five minutes, make a stop at 5 metres/15 feet for at least 15 minutes (air supply allowing) and do not dive for at least 24 hours.

By double-checking your computer and/or reviewing the RDP during your safety stop and by having emergency breathing equipment available, you're not likely to accidentally omit an emergency decompression stop. If it were to happen, however, remain calm. Tell your buddies or the divemaster and monitor yourself closely for symptoms of decompression sickness. Breathe 100 percent oxygen if available. If anything unusual develops, seek medical assistance.

Do *not* reenter the water. The old U.S. Navy procedures for omitted decompression are not recommended for recreational divers. The amount of air and support required may work for military and technical divers, but they're not suitable for a recreational diver.

For example, U.S. Navy omitted decompression procedures for a 21 metre/70 foot dive call for 21 minutes decompression beginning at 12 metres/40 feet. Assuming you didn't have decompression sickness symptoms, you would need to calculate the emergency decompression, change cylinders - if necessary, and *if* you have one - and then reenter the water - all within *five minutes!* Additionally, you have to consider other factors, such as the water temperature, your exposure protection and how cold you already are.

The Navy procedures were based on a diver having surface-supplied air, a helmet or full-face mask, and the presence of a chamber on site, all of which aren't likely in recreational diving situations.

Required Safety Stop/Decompression Stop: The Difference

Because the Recreational Dive Planner lists instances when a safety stop is required, some divers ask: "If a safety stop is *required*, how does it differ from an emergency decompression stop?"

The answer lies in the diver's decompression situation, and why the stop is required: When a required safety stop is called for, the diver is still within the limits of the decompression model. The stop is required procedurally for conservatism because the diver has neared the limits.

When a true "decompression stop" is called for, the diver has exceeded the limits of the decompression model. This is more serious, because the diver has more nitrogen than the maximums allowed by the decompression model. If the diver were to skip the stop and surface, he would face an unacceptably high risk of decompression sickness. The decompression stop is necessary so the diver releases excess nitrogen before surfacing, returning him to acceptable levels. In short, a required safety stop keeps a diver well within decompression limits, while a decompression stop returns a diver from outside the limits.

Deep Stops

In the past few years, the development of *bubble dynamics decompression modeling* has brought with it some new thinking about how bubbles form within the body and how the body deals with those bubbles. These new concepts suggest that the body eliminates excess nitrogen more effectively if we make deeper safety and decompression stops.

With respect to no stop recreational diving, a growing number of divers now make a deep safety stop for one to three minutes at 12 metres/40 feet when they have been diving deeper than 18 metres/60 feet. This is in *addition* to the three to five minute safety stop at 5 metres/15 feet.

Provided this extra stop does not put you over your dive computer or RDP limits (it shouldn't if you're diving well within limits), there's nothing wrong with making a deep safety stop in addition to the conventional one.

Exercise 7 – Deep Diving Techniques: Safety Stops and Emergency Decompression

1. When making a safety stop, you should maintain your _____ at 5 metres/15 feet.

    ☐ a. face

    ☐ b. chest

    ☐ c. waist

2. If you accidentally omit an emergency decompression stop, you should

    ☐ a. return to the water and make the stop.

    ☐ b. remain out of the water and monitor yourself for DCS symptoms.

How'd you do?
1. b. 2. b.

Deep Diving Techniques:
Drift Dives and Wall Dives

Two common types of deep dives call for special considerations beyond what you've learned so far. These are *drift dives* and *wall dives*. A drift dive is one in which you enter the water and float with the current, often followed by a boat, and then exit the water down current. A wall dive is a dive made along a sheer vertical drop-off, which may plunge hundreds of metres/feet deep.

Study Objectives

Underline/highlight the answers to these questions as you read:

1. What are five recommended guidelines to follow when making a deep drift dive?

2. What's a wall dive, and what three recommended guidelines should you follow when making a deep wall dive?

Deep Drift Dives

One of the main advantages of drift diving is that it's usually relaxing, which certainly makes it a suitable form of deep diving. However, deep drift dives do require some coordination. If you've never made a drift dive, it's recommended that you begin with shallow drift dives, preferably supervised by a PADI Instructor, before making deep drift dives. A good place to start is with a Drift Adventure Dive as part of the Adventures in Diving program.

For deep drift dives, keep these five recommendations in mind:

1. Although you can drift dive from shore in many areas, it's preferable to make deep drift dives from a boat. With a boat, you don't have to worry about overshooting your exit point.

2. Because you're entering moving water, you need to be closely coordinated with your buddy. On a deep dive, you won't have time to regroup if you get separated (usually you have to end the dive), so you want to start and stay together. Do everything at the same time as your buddy – suit up, enter, descend and ascend.

3. Depending on the location, you may enter the water with an inflated BCD or you may enter the water with an empty BCD and descend immediately. When diving with a group, it's important that everyone agrees on and uses the same technique. This keeps the group together. Currents usually move faster at the surface than at depth, so if divers descend at different rates, they may become separated. Groups should generally come up together, too.

4. When possible, tow an unanchored line and buoy as a visual reference for the trailing boat and for ascents. During the dive, make sure your equipment is streamlined and secured. Dangling equipment on a drift dive can be hazardous to you and the environment. It can snag on exposed features of the site preventing you from safely moving forward and it can destroy aquatic life in an instant or break off exposed parts of shipwrecks. Ascend near the float ball, first to keep the group together, and second because the float identifies your location for boaters. Nonetheless, surface with caution, watching and listening for boats.

5. Watch your air supply and no stop times closely and allow an extra margin with both. On drift dives it's often impractical to have emergency breathing equipment hanging from the boat or buoy. You may therefore want to allow an extra air reserve to assure you can make your safety stop.

When making deep drift dives, it's often impractical to have emergency breathing equipment hanging from the boat or buoy. You may therefore want to allow an extra air reserve to assure you can make your safety stop.

Accessories and Davy Jones' Locker

On many deep dives, but especially along walls, if you drop something it's probably gone. Accordingly, use wrist lanyards or clips as appropriate to keep from dropping things, especially expensive accessories like photo equipment.

If you do accidentally drop something, let it go. Don't chase it. It may be painful to lose something expensive like a camera, but it's not worth your health or safety. If something means so much to you that you couldn't sacrifice it to stay safe, leave it at home.

For Want of an Attitude

There's a piece of folk lore that goes, "For want of a nail, the horseshoe was lost. For want of a horseshoe, the horse was lost. For want of a horse, the soldier was lost. For want of a soldier, the battle was lost. For want of a battle, the war was lost. For want of the war, the kingdom was lost."

The moral is that small acts can snowball into big consequences, and that's certainly true in deep diving. That's why it's important that you and any buddies you deep dive with maintain an appropriate *attitude* regarding deep diving. Namely, that recreational deep diving remains fun and has acceptable risk only as long as you apply appropriate principles and techniques, including those you've learned in this course. When you disregard proper procedures, fun and safety go out the window. Here's a realistic example of how little things can go awry.

Paula and Mike were diving along the top of a wall at 24 metres/80 feet. Neither of them had mentioned anything in the way of a dive plan; their usual practice was to signal "up" when their SPG hit the caution zone.

They had been down for 24 minutes, when Mike noticed that they had drifted well down current from the line the boat was moored to. He signaled Paula, and both began swimming against the current. Both had to swim hard because the current was stronger than they realized.

Just as they reached the line, Mike signaled out-of-air. They fumbled until Paula located her alternate air source, which had snagged on her cylinder band. Mike got it in his mouth, cleared it and began breathing. Unfortunately, it was very hard to breathe from. Feeling air starved, he began to panic. Paula had to calm him down and get him to slow his breathing. All this delayed their ascent about a minute.

They were just over halfway to the surface when Paula ran out of air, too. They just managed to kick frantically to the surface; fortunately, both remembered to exhale all the way to the surface. The ascent exceeded a safe rate, and of course they made no safety stop. The chase boat picked them up, and 20 minutes later, they were back aboard, miserable, but fortunate not to have decompression illness or worse, which would not have been surprising.

What did Paula and Mike do wrong? They:

- failed to evaluate conditions.
- failed to plan an appropriate reserve.
- failed to monitor SPG frequently, especially during hard work.
- failed to properly secure and maintain an alternate air source.

Note that not one of these caused the incident, but all contributed to a chain reaction. Any one of these would have probably prevented or stopped the incident. If they had evaluated conditions, they would have known about the current. If they had had an appropriate reserve, they could have handled the current, even if they didn't realize it was there until too late. If Mike had watched his SPG, they could have ascended while he had air and be picked up by the chase boat. If Paula had taken care of her alternate air source, they could have made a safe ascent on the line.

Therefore, fun and risk management in diving, especially deep diving, lie in following all the appropriate procedures to the best of your ability. When you do, a mistake doesn't have to lead to an incident or accident.

So, one day you may accidentally find yourself downstream because you failed to notice a current. If you've stuck with the principles of safe, conservative diving, you and your buddy should be able to handle it with little difficulty. If you haven't, well, for want of a nail. . . .

Deep Wall Dives

Deep dives along walls are exhilarating, especially in very clear water. When making a dive along a "bottomless" wall, there are three considerations, the most important of which is to watch your depth. In clear water especially, it's easy to drift down and exceed depth limits without realizing it.

The second is to try to dive close to the wall so you can use it as a reference. You're more likely to experience vertigo if you're away from the wall in midwater.

 However, leave enough space to avoid damaging any aquatic life on the wall. Aquatic organisms on walls are spectacularly beautiful, but mostly very fragile. The idea is to be near the wall, but not close enough to harm it by bumping into it.

Finally, if a wall reaches near the surface, you can use it as a natural reference, eliminating a need for a reference line. In such instances, you can make a safety stop at the top of the wall, or just over the reef edge at 5 metres/15 feet.

Try to dive close to a wall, but leave enough room to avoid damaging fragile aquatic life.

Ten Ways a Diver Can Protect the Underwater Environment

Deep drift dives and diving deep-water walls are some of the most exhilarating dives. Be cognizant of how your interactions with the environment affect aquatic life. It's important to adhere to these tips to protect the underwater environment:

1. Dive carefully to protect fragile aquatic ecosystems.

2. Be aware of your body and equipment placement when diving.

3. Keep your dive skills sharp through continuing education.

4. Consider how your interactions affect aquatic life.

5. Understand and respect underwater life.

6. Be an ecotourist.

7. Respect underwater cultural heritage.

8. Report environmental disturbances or destruction.

9. Be a role model for other divers and nondivers when interacting with the environment.

10. Get involved in local environmental activities and issues.

You can download the complete *Project AWARE Foundation* brochure *"Ten Ways a Diver Can Protect the Underwater Environment"* located at

http://www.projectaware.org/americas/english/pdfs/AW_TenWays.pdf .

Exercise 8 – Deep Diving Techniques: Drift Dives and Wall Dives

1. The recommendations for making a deep drift dive generally include (check all that apply):

   ☐ a. watching for boats when you surface.

   ☐ b. towing a float.

   ☐ c. swimming against the current as much as possible.

   ☐ d. descending and ascending together.

2. When making a wall dive, you should stay as far from the wall as possible.

   ☐ True   ☐ False

How'd you do?

1. a, b, d. Not "c" because you float with the current on a drift dive.
2. False. You should stay near the wall to use it as a reference, but avoid touching it and damaging aquatic life.

Gas *Narcosis*

Study Objectives

Underline/highlight the answers to these questions as you read:

1. At approximately what depth does narcosis typically begin to affect divers?

2. What are seven symptoms and four signs of narcosis?

3. What five factors may speed the onset of, or intensify the effects of narcosis?

4. In recreational diving, how do you prevent narcosis, and what do you do if it occurs?

In your PADI Open Water Diver course, you learned a bit about *nitrogen narcosis* (or more properly, *gas narcosis*), which is the narcotic property of air or enriched air when breathed under pressure on deep dives. As a PADI Deep Diver, you'll be making dives into the narcosis depth range, so it's important to have more insight into the phenomenon.

Presently physiologists don't understand the exact causes of nitrogen narcosis, but it has been linked to absorption of nitrogen into nerve cell structure. The most accepted hypothesis (Meyer-Overton hypothesis) states that *all* gases (including oxygen - hence the preferred term *gas narcosis*) can induce narcosis if they penetrate the cell lipid (fat) structure in sufficient concentration. The gas interferes with the transmission of nerve impulses from one nerve cell to the next. Other factors, such as the presence of carbon dioxide, appear to contribute to narcosis, though physiologists still don't fully understand all the mechanisms and their interactions.

Generally speaking, the more soluble a gas is in liquid, the more narcotic it is. For example, nitrous oxide (laughing gas) is highly soluble and highly narcotic at surface pressure. This is why dentists use it as an anesthetic. Helium, on the other hand, has much less solubility than nitrogen. Commercial and technical divers use helium mixes for extremely deep diving to avoid or reduce nitrogen narcosis. (However, note that in exchange for reduced narcosis helium poses other potential risks and problems, which is why you need specialized training in commercial or deep tec diving before diving with helium gas blends.)

Because narcosis is a physiological phenomenon, it is variable depending upon the individual, and upon physical condition. This means it not only varies from person to person, but in the same person from day to day. Nevertheless, as a rule of thumb, most divers begin to find the effects of narcosis noticeable at approximately 30 metres/100 feet. This doesn't mean that the effect is severe, but it is usually present. During your Deep Diver training dives, you'll be able to measure how narcosis affects you by performing a timed task at the surface, and then again underwater. At depth, it's likely to take a bit longer to do the same task.

Narcosis is a physiological phenomenon, which means its effect not only vary from person to person, but can vary with the same person on different dives.

Learn more *see* The Encyclopedia of Recreational Diving, *The Physiology of Diving*

Narcosis itself is harmless. The hazard is that a strongly affected diver might act inappropriately, such as fail to monitor depth and time. A "narked" diver may react slowly or not at all in an emergency. On deep dives, it's important to be alert for the signs and symptoms of strong narcosis.

The common *signs* (what you observe in another diver) include:

- Inappropriate behavior, such as poor diving habits.

- Short attention span and slowed thinking, such as having trouble understanding a dive computer or hand signals.

- Impaired vigilance and a disregard for safety.

- Stupor and semi consciousness.

The common symptoms (what you feel yourself) include:

- Rigid, inflexible thinking, such as being unable to adapt to unexpected conditions on a dive.

- Loss of good judgment and short-term memory loss.

- A false sense of security.

- Lack of concern for a specific task or for your own safety.

- Unjustified elation.

- Drowsiness and a desire to sleep.

- Anxiety.

Because narcosis is a form of intoxication, physiological conditions can intensify it. These include:

- Hard work underwater and/or failure to breathe deeply, which builds up carbon dioxide levels.

- Inexperience with deep diving or no recent deep dives. Divers with deep diving experience seem to build a temporary adaptation to and compensation for narcosis.

- Alcohol or drugs (tranquilizers, barbiturates, sleeping pills, some decongestants, etc.) that cause drowsiness. These chemicals impair nerve impulse transmission, so that when combined with nitrogen, narcosis can occur at surprisingly shallow depths. It's understood that you never dive whilst under the influence of alcohol and that you use prescription drugs only with the clearance from a doctor.

- Anxiety. Anxiety creates perceptual narrowing and other psychological reactions that can magnify the effects of narcosis. Low visibility, cold and dark water can all contribute to anxiety, and therefore narcosis.

- Fatigue. Just as alcohol and other intoxicants affect you more when you're tired, so does breathing a gas under pressure. If you're tired, you're more likely to have narcosis affect you.

Don't ignore narcosis, even if you or an apparently affected diver seems able to handle routine tasks. Such a diver may be able to dive adequately, but may not be able to respond properly to an emergency.

By ascending to shallower depths, narcosis will subside on its own with no aftereffects. Most of the time you can avoid narcosis by staying above 30 metres/100 feet, keeping in mind that it can occur at shallower depths.

Exercise 9 – Gas Narcosis

1. As a general rule, divers can expect to be affected by narcosis at approximately

   ☐ a. 18 metres/60 feet.

   ☐ b. 30 metres/100 feet.

   ☐ c. 40 metres/130 feet.

2. Signs and symptoms of narcosis include (check all that apply):

   ☐ a. lack of concern for safety.

   ☐ b. limb and joint pain.

   ☐ c. inappropriate behavior.

   ☐ d. anxiety.

   ☐ e. hyperactivity.

3. Factors that may increase the effects of narcosis include (check all that apply):

   ☐ a. alcohol and drugs.

   ☐ b. fatigue.

   ☐ c. helium.

   ☐ d. frequent deep dives.

4. A diver experiencing narcosis should

   ☐ a. ascend to a shallower depth, where the symptoms will disappear on their own.

   ☐ b. leave the water and seek recompression.

How'd you do?
1. b. 2. a, c, d. Not "b" or "e" these are not narcosis symptoms. 3. a, b. Not "c" because helium is used by professional (nonrecreational) divers to reduce narcosis. Not "d" because frequent deep diving doesn't make narcosis more likely. 4. a.

Decompression Sickness

Study Objectives

Underline/highlight the answers to these questions as you read:

1. What is the primary reason recreational divers experience decompression sickness?

2. What are six symptoms and six signs of decompression sickness?

3. What ten factors may predispose a diver toward decompression sickness?

4. What can you do to avoid decompression sickness?

5. What is the recommended emergency care for a diver suspected of having decompression sickness?

6. What are seven reasons why a diver suspected of having decompression sickness should not be recompressed underwater?

Many of the procedures recommended for deep diving and diving in general are intended to help you avoid decompression sickness (DCS). As you learned in your PADI Open Water Diver class, decompression sickness - sometimes called "the bends" - results from excess nitrogen dissolved in the body forming bubbles when critical levels have been exceeded.

While there's always some minimal possibility that DCS will occur, even when you do everything right, you should be aware that the *primary* reason divers suffer DCS is from *diver error*. These errors cause a diver to absorb more nitrogen than expected, or fail to release sufficient nitrogen safely before surfacing. These errors include misuse of, or failure to use dive computers or tables, exceeding proper ascent rates, omitting emergency decompression stops, running out of air (which can lead to exceeding proper ascent rates and omitting emergency decompression/safety stops), ignoring factors that predispose divers to DCS, and failure to follow conservative diving practices (such as staying well within your computer's limits).

A diver suffering from DCS may show various signs and experience various symptoms, depending upon where in the body bubbles form. Signs include:

- Favoring an arm or leg, or rubbing a joint
- Paralysis
- Unconsciousness
- Staggering
- Collapse
- Coughing spasms
- Blotchy skin rash

Learn more *see* The Encyclopedia of Recreational Diving, *The Physiology of Diving*

Learn more *see* The PADI Rescue Diver Manual

Symptoms include:

- Pain, often in the limbs, and also often, but not necessarily in the joints. The pain can move over time.
- Numbness, tingling or paralysis
- Unusual fatigue or weakness
- Skin itch
- Shortness of breath
- Dizziness and Vertigo

In the majority of instances, DCS occurs at the surface within one to two hours of the dive. However, it can occur underwater at a shallow depth, and symptoms can be delayed as long as 48 hours. Furthermore, DCS may become more likely based on these factors:

- Dehydration. This reduces the quantity of blood circulating to eliminate nitrogen.
- Excess fat tissue and poor fitness. Fat tissue holds more dissolved nitrogen, and being out of shape impairs circulatory and respiratory efficiency. It also reduces tolerances to physical stressors.
- Age. As a person ages, the circulatory system becomes less efficient, therefore in theory, nitrogen elimination slows. However, studies show mixed results when comparing age to DCS incidence. People also tend to have more fat tissue as they get older, so age-related concerns may be more related to fitness than age.
- Heavy exertion immediately before, during or immediately after a deep dive. Exertion before or after the dive can promote micro bubbles that grow as excess nitrogen dissolves into them. Exertion during the dive speeds up the circulation, accumulating more nitrogen than normal.
- Injuries and illness. These can affect circulation and the ability to eliminate nitrogen.

- Use of alcohol. Before the dive, this can cause dehydration, and immediately after the dive it alters circulation, possibly promoting bubble growth.

- Cold water. To save heat, the body restricts circulation to parts of the body, thereby eliminating nitrogen less effectively.

- Hot showers or baths immediately after a dive. These cause skin capillaries to dilate, altering circulation.

- Carbon dioxide increase. This is usually caused by exertion or skip-breathing (breath holding) and interferes with the blood's ability to carry nitrogen.

- Exposure to altitude. Flying or driving to altitude after diving or diving at altitude require special guidelines because dive computers and tables base their calculations on surfacing at sea level. Altitude exposures lessen the surrounding pressure after a dive, allowing bubbles to form when they wouldn't be expected at sea level. Follow current recommendations when flying or driving to altitude after diving. If you'll be diving at altitude, get the proper training in the PADI Altitude Diver Specialty course.

To prevent DCS, adhere to safe, conservative diving practices. Stay well within the limits of your dive computer or table, and make safety stops at the end of every dive.

It's important to remember that because people differ in their susceptibility to decompression sickness, no computer or decompression table can guarantee that decompression sickness will never occur, even though you dive within the table or computer limits. Physiologists can point to predisposing factors, but presently, there's no way to quantify them in such a way that they can be incorporated into a decompression model. Therefore, the more predisposing factors that apply to you, the more important it is to dive conservatively.

Jet Lag and Diving

Compare the symptoms of prolonged air travel to the decompression sickness predisposing factors, and you come up with some significant matches:

- Dehydration – Aircraft air is very dry, and you lose more fluid just sitting there than you may realize. Of course, the polite flight attendants offer you plenty of coffee, which is a diuretic and therefore, you lose even more fluid.

- Alcohol use – Okay, you're on vacation, but remember, alcohol is a diuretic, too. It dehydrates you.

- Illness – Before you protest that you're not sick, be honest. You have a sleepless overnight flight across four time zones, despite, perhaps, a couple of cocktails to help you doze off. An hour before the plane lands, you slug back two cups of coffee to stay awake. After you arrive, you either roast or freeze because you're dressed for where you started, not for where you are now. By the time you get to the hotel, you're walking around in a fatigued daze because your body has suddenly remembered that it's three a.m. – Do you recall that well?

If the rigors of air travel leave you exhausted and dehydrated, use your arrival day to catch up. Get plenty of sleep and rehydrate by drinking plenty of noncaffeinated, nonalcoholic beverages, like fruit juices or water. You'll enjoy your dives more by diving refreshed and reduce the predisposing factors at the same time.

Emergency Care for Decompression Sickness

If a diver is suspected of decompression sickness, and you're not diving with professional supervision, such as on a charter boat, you should know the steps to take.

Have the diver lie down and administer 100 percent oxygen if available. Oxygen helps eliminate nitrogen and it raises the blood oxygen level to assist tissues receiving less than normal due to bubble blockage. For most cases, have the diver lie on the back or left side, whichever is more comfortable, but not sitting up.

In severe cases, in which the patient has no breath and no signs of circulation, you will need to provide CPR. In this case, the patient must be face up. Put an unresponsive breathing diver in the recovery position, left side down. (If you're not yet familiar with CPR and first aid, ask your instructor about the Emergency First Response Primary Care and Secondary Care courses.)

After beginning first aid - or *before* if the diver is unresponsive and you're alone - immediately contact the local emergency medical system. In many areas, specialized diver emergency networks can assist you and local medical personnel in locating a chamber and consult in treating the diver.

Have a diver suspected of having DCS lie back down or left side down and breathe oxygen at the highest possible concentration, ideally 100 percent.

About DAN International

International DAN (IDAN) is comprised of several independent DAN organizations based around the world to provide expert emergency medical and referral services to regional diving communities. Each IDAN organization is a nonprofit, independently administered organization.

The International Divers Alert Network (IDAN) provides this service in North America, Central America, South America and the Caribbean.

In Europe, regions of coverage include geographical Europe, the countries of the Mediterranean Basin, the countries on the shores of the Red Sea, the Middle East including the Persian Gulf, the countries on the shores of the Indian Ocean north of the Equator and West of India and Sri Lanka, as well as the related overseas territories, districts, and protectorates.

DAN Japan regions include Japan, Japanese Islands, and related territories.

Asia-Pacific regions of coverage include all Asian countries between India and Korea, Australia, New Zealand, and the South Pacific Islands.

DAN Southern Africa regions of coverage include South Africa, Swaziland, Lesotho, Namibia, Botswana, Zimbabwe, Mozambique, Angola, Zambia, Malawi, Tanzania, Kenya, Madagascar, Comoros, Seychelles, and Mauritius.

For more information about DAN, refer to http://www.diversalertnetwork.org.

49

Secondary medical treatment for DCS usually requires recompression in a chamber. Recompression reduces the bubbles and forces them back into solution. Then, accompanied by oxygen, drug therapy and fluids for rehydration, the diver is brought back to surface pressure at a slow, controlled rate. Often, more than one recompression is required.

Recompression Chambers

Divers who have never seen a recompression chamber often have little idea of what "a chamber" is like. While they vary in size from barely larger than a human to apartment-sized complexes, here's a description of a "standard" recompression chamber:

The chamber is a horizontal steel cylinder, usually 3 metres/10 feet to 5.5 metres/18 feet long and 1.5 metres/5 feet to 2.4 metres/8 feet in diameter. At one or both ends, there's a pressure tight circular or oval hatch. On one side, there's a large bank of instruments and dials for controlling the chamber.

Inside, there's a primary chamber, with one or more patient beds, and a secondary chamber that allows medical personnel to lock in and out of the main chamber. With interior flooring and mats, there's usually insufficient headroom to stand up fully.

An air compressor and air banks pressurize the chamber, usually to a maximum of 50 metres/165 feet of pressure. During the treatment, chamber operators lower the pressure, and periodically refresh the air by carefully adding and venting air.

A chamber treatment follows a set of treatment tables, similar to dive tables, although much longer. Usually the patient breathes oxygen for part of the treatment. Rather than fill the entire chamber with pure oxygen (which can create a fire hazard), the patient breathes from a mask or hood, with excess pure oxygen channeled safely out of the chamber.

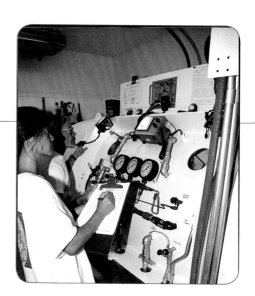

Decompression Sickness, Decompression Illness

In diving medical circles and in the PADI Rescue Diver course, you'll hear the terms "decompression sickness," "arterial gas embolism" and "decompression illness." They're similar, but not necessarily identical terms.

"Decompression sickness" is the malady caused by excess nitrogen (or other inert gas in commercial or technical diving) coming out of solution in the blood stream and other body tissues. "Arterial gas embolism," also called "AGE" and "air embolism" is the injury caused by lung overexpansion when a diver ascends holding his breath or experiences air trapping in the lungs (such as mucus blockage due to diving with a cold). The lung ruptures, releasing bubbles into the arterial blood flow.

In both cases, once in the blood stream and tissues, the bubbles may block blood flow and deprive tissues of oxygen.

"Decompression illness" is a clinical term for both decompression sickness and arterial gas embolism. The reason is that decompression sickness and arterial gas embolism, while having different causes, have similar signs and symptoms, and require the same first aid and treatment. At an accident scene, it's not important to distinguish between the two, so we use a single term. In fact, it is often clinically impossible to distinguish between the two.

To learn more about handling diving emergencies, including decompression illness, enroll in two courses: first, the Emergency First Response program, which teaches you first aid and CPR appropriate for responding to both nondiving and diving emergencies, and second, the PADI Rescue Diver and Emergency Oxygen Provider Courses, which focus on diving, and develops your ability to prevent and handle diving accidents. Completing these makes you much more prepared for dive emergencies, and can be especially important when you dive in remote areas.

In old movies and television shows, "bent" divers recompressed by going back underwater. In reality, this isn't a good idea, for several reasons: Recompression often requires extreme pressure - the equivalent of 50 metres/165 feet, which is well beyond safe diving depths. Recompression usually involves oxygen and drug therapy, both of which are at best difficult and under many circumstances impossible underwater. Recompression treatments typically take six to 10 hours - far longer than a diver can reasonably endure the heat loss even in very warm water, and that assumes having adequate air for such a dive. Attempting treatment underwater makes it impossible for medical personnel to observe the diver, and the diver's safety is jeopardized because it's hard to communicate with the diver. Finally, and perhaps the most important, is that attempting to recompress underwater will make someone worse if with an incomplete attempt, and it only delays getting the patient to a proper medical facility.

Exercise 10 – Decompression Sickness

1. The primary reason divers suffer from decompression sickness is:

   ☐ a. statistical inevitability.

   ☐ b. diver error.

2. The signs and symptoms of decompression sickness include (check all that apply):

   ☐ a. limb pain.

   ☐ b. blotchy skin.

   ☐ c. lack of concern for safety.

   ☐ d. paralysis.

3. Factors that may predispose a diver to decompression sickness include (check all that apply):

   ☐ a. excess fat tissue.

   ☐ b. dehydration.

   ☐ c. prolonged safety stops.

   ☐ d. alcohol consumption.

4. To avoid decompression sickness, you should (check all that apply):

   ☐ a. dive well within table/computer limits.

   ☐ b. make safety stops.

   ☐ c. adhere to conservative diving practices.

5. A diver suspected of having decompression sickness

   ☐ a. should lie down and be given 100 percent oxygen.

   ☐ b. should return to the water to recompress.

How'd you do?
1. b. *2.* a, b, d. Not "c" which is a symptom of gas narcosis. *3.* a, b, d. Not "c" because safety stops reduce the probability of decompression sickness. *4.* a, b, c. *5.* a.

Deep Diving and Responsibility

When you've successfully completed the PADI Deep Diver Specialty course, you'll have the knowledge and skills for fun and adventure exploring deeper dive sites. As time passes, maintain your proficiency by rereading this manual and rewatching the PADI *Deep Diving* video, especially if it's been a while since your last deep dive.

A final thought: It's been said that one who disregards knowledge is a greater fool than one who lacks knowledge. So, as a diver your responsibility calls for more than knowing appropriate deep diving techniques. It calls for applying what you know when you deep dive, and staying within the limits of your training and qualifications. If diving beyond recreational limits (40 metres/130 feet and/or the no stop limits) is a challenge that interests you, do it right - get trained as a DSAT Tec Deep Diver.

Deep Diver Specialty Course
Open Water Dives

The following outlines the four dives you'll make as part of your PADI Deep Diver Specialty course. Your instructor may rearrange skill sequences in each dive, or may add more dives as necessary to meet your needs, desires, course requirements and the environmental conditions. Note: During your open water dives, you'll most likely be using a dive computer and the Recreational Dive Planner, either the Table, or the eRDPML.

Dive 1

- Knowledge Review/Briefing
- Predive Procedures – Above Water Skill Practice
- Dive 1 Tasks
    - Execute a descent using a reference as a tactile or visual guide (line, wall or sloping bottom).
    - Compare your own depth gauge to your instructor's and/or other student diver's depth gauges.
    - Describe and record changes of colors at depth.
    - Use a depth gauge and timing device (or a dive computer with an ascent-rate indicator) to measure an ascent rate not to exceed 18 metres/60 feet per minute.
    - Perform a 3-minute safety stop at 5 metres/15 feet before surfacing.
- Post-dive Procedures
- Debrief
- Log Dive

Dive 2

- Knowledge Review/Briefing
- Predive Procedures – Above Water Skill Practice
- Dive 2 Tasks
    - Execute a "free" descent using a reference line, wall or sloping bottom as a visual guide only.
    - Describe and record the changes that occur to three pressure-sensitive items while at depth.
    - Perform a navigation swim with a compass away from, and back to, the anchor of the reference line (one diver navigates away from, the other navigates back to, the reference line for a distance of between 10 and 20 kick cycles, depending on visibility).
    - Perform an ascent using a reference line, wall or sloping bottom as a visual guide only.
    - Use depth gauge and timing device (or a dive computer with ascent-rate indicator) to measure an ascent rate not to exceed 18 metres/60 feet per minute.

- Perform a 3-minute safety stop at 5 metres/15 feet before surfacing without physically holding on to a reference line for positioning.
- Post-dive Procedures
- Debrief
- Log Dive

Dive 3

- Knowledge Review/Briefing
- Predive Procedures – Above Water Skill Practice
- Dive 3 Tasks
    - Execute a descent using a reference as a tactile or visual guide (line, wall or sloping bottom).
    - Compare the amount of time needed to complete a task on the surface and at depth.
    - Perform an ascent using a reference as a tactile or visual guide (line, wall or sloping bottom).
    - Use a depth gauge and timing device (or a dive computer with ascent-rate indicator) to measure an ascent rate not to exceed 18 metres/60 feet per minute.
    - Perform an 8-minute simulated emergency decompression stop at 5 metres/15 feet before surfacing, while breathing from an emergency air source for at least one minute of the total time.
- Post-dive Procedures
- Debrief
- Log Dive

Dive 4

- Knowledge Review/Briefing
- Predive Procedures – Above Water Skill Practice
- Dive 4 Tasks
    - Execute a descent using a reference as a tactile or visual guide (line, wall or sloping bottom).
    - Complete an underwater tour of the area.
    - Perform an ascent using a reference as a tactile or visual guide (line, wall or sloping bottom).
    - Use your depth gauge and timing device (or a dive computer with ascent-rate indicator) to measure an ascent rate not to exceed 18 metres/60 feet per minute.
    - Perform a 3-minute safety stop at 5 metres/15 feet before surfacing.
- Post-dive Procedures
- Debrief
- Log Dive

Name <u>Carrie Dungan</u> Date <u>22 april 2022</u>

Knowledge Review — Part I

Note to the student: The first half of this Knowledge Review is the same Knowledge Review in the Deep Diving section of Adventures in Diving. If your instructor has the first half on file from your PADI Adventure Diver or PADI Advanced Open Water Diver course, your instructor may have you complete only the second half of this Knowledge Review.

Answer the following questions and bring this completed Knowledge Review with you to your next training session.

1. List five factors to consider when determining your personal deep-diving depth limit.

   1. <u>The environment</u>
   2. <u>Yourself</u>
   3. <u>Previous dives</u>
   4. <u>Proximity of emergency care</u>
   5. <u>Your buddy</u>

2. Explain how to determine if your equipment is suitable for deep diving.

   Make sure it's working properly, is serviced regularly, and you have a balanced regulator.

3. List five pieces of specialized equipment recommended for deep diving.

   1. <u>reference line</u>
   2. <u>emergency breathing equipment</u>
   3. <u>extra weight</u>
   4. <u>dive light</u>
   5. <u>~~support stations~~ first aid kit + emergency O_2</u>

4. Describe proper ascent and descent techniques for deep diving, including positioning, maintaining a proper ascent rate and descending/ascending without a visual reference.

   Head up, maintain neutral bouyancy.   60 ft/18m per minute   monitor rate/
   w/o reference line: head up, eye contact w/ buddy, watch computer, make safety stop when going up.

55

5. Explain how to avoid low-on-air or out-of-air situations while deep diving.

Check your SPG frequently, + relax, + have reserve

watching reference pt or/and computer

6. Describe how to make a safety stop at 5 metres/15 feet with a visual reference (line, wall, or sloping bottom).

ascend until you reach 5m, adjusting bouyancy properly, remain w/ chest near 5m for 3-5min, head up

7. Describe how to prevent narcosis, and how to treat it if it occurs.

Ascend. Hydrate. Stay fit. Don't over exert yourself. avoid alcohol/drugs.
Reduce anxiety. Be well rested.
if it occurs.

8. List six symptoms and six signs of decompression illness.

Symptoms	Signs
1. Rigid thinking	1. inappropriate behavior
2. loss of good judgement	2. slowed thinking
3. false sense of security	3. short attention span
4. lack of concern	4. impaired vigilance
5. unjustified elation	5. disregard for safety
6. drowsiness	6. stupor

9. What is the primary reason divers get decompression illness?

Diver error - failure to use computer, exceeding proper ascent rates, omitting no deco stops, running out of air

10. Explain how to minimize the risk of decompression illness.

Adhere to safe, conservative diving practices; stay within limits + make safety stops

Student Diver Statement:

Any questions I answered incorrectly or incompletely, I've had explained to me, and I understand what I missed.

Name _Carrie Dingan_____ Date _22 April 2022_

Name _Carrie Dungan_ Date _22 April 2022_

Knowledge Review — Part II

Answer the following questions and bring this completed Knowledge Review with you to your next training session.

11. Describe a proper deep diving objective:

Nearly singular and specific

KISS — keep it simple, stupid

12. List five guidelines to follow when using a dive computer:

1. Always use as no stop dive
2. Don't share computers
3. Follow the most conservative
4. in case of failure, ascend safely + safety stop
5. compare w/ others computers

13. Describe how to maintain neutral buoyancy while deep diving.

add air while descending, release air while ascending

14. Describe two techniques for estimating a proper ascent rate.

ascend along a line, use a sloping wall for reference   1)
2) use dive computer
look up

15. Explain what divers should do if they discover they have accidentally omitted an emergency decompression stop:

~~Extend stop time to cover no deco requirements~~
lie down, O_2, monitor, seek EM care, don't re enter water
8 mins @ 5m if you exceeded up to 5m, 15min if are exceeded greater than 5min

16. List five recommendations that you should follow when making a deep drift dive.

1. From a boat ideally
2. closely coordinate w/ buddy
3. clarify positive/negative entry technique
4. tow unanchored line + bouy for reference
5. watch air + no stop times - allow extra margains

17. List four guidelines you should follow when diving near a wall:

    1. watch depth
    2. dive close to wall
    3. avoid damaging aquatic life
    4. use as natural reference

18. List ten factors that may predispose a diver to decompression sickness.

    1. Dehydration
    2. poor fitness
    3. alcohol/drugs
    4. heavy exertion
    5. age
    6. illness or injury
    7. cold water
    8. hot shower/bath after
    9. CO_2 ↑
    10. exposure to altitude

19. Describe the steps to take if a diver is suspected of having decompression sickness.

    lie down, give 100% oxygen. Provide CPR if necessary
    Get to EMS ASAP for recompression chamber.

20. Explain why a diver suspected of having decompression sickness should not be put

back in the water.

    Extreme pressure is required- more than within safe diving limits.
    Need it w/ oxygen + drugs + monitoring. Can take 6-10 hours.
    Can make them worse + delay getting to EMS.

Student Diver Statement:

Any questions I answered incorrectly or incompletely, I've had explained to me, and I understand what I missed.

Name _Carrie Dingan_

Date _22 april 2022_

PADI courses have the unique distinction of meeting academic excellence criteria as established by university and vocational accreditation bodies. Find out how you can get credit for your PADI education!

Australia

PADI Divers may receive credit toward various certificates and diplomas for several PADI courses within the Australian national training system. The following training providers recognise certain PADI and Emergency First Response® (EFR) courses — Technical and Further Education, South Australia; Australia Fisheries Academy, South Australia; Victorian Tertiary Admissions Center, Victoria; and the Western Australia Curriculum Council. For more information, go to: www.padi.com/scuba/scuba-diving-guide/start-scuba-diving/scuba-lessons-for-college-credit/default.aspx.

Canada

The British Columbia Ministry of Education (External Credentials Program for Industrial and Occupational Courses) has approved the PADI Open Water Diver (2 credits), PADI Advanced Open Water or Adventures in Diving Program (4 credits) and PADI Rescue Diver (4 credits) courses for school credit. Grade 10, 11 and 12 students who have been certified in these PADI courses simply present their PADI certification card to the school administration to apply for credit. For information on receiving credit contact your school's administration. On an individual, merit-base case, divers in Canada may also receive credit for PADI courses through the USA-based American Council on Education's College Credit Recommendation Service as noted under "United States."

England, Wales and Northern Ireland

PADI Open Water Scuba Instructors can apply to PADI for the Certificate in Scuba Instruction, a Vocationally Related Qualification (VRQ) accredited at Level 3 on the National Qualifications Framework in England, Wales and Northern Ireland, by the Qualifications and Curriculum Authority (QCA) for England, Department for Education, Lifelong Learning and Skills (DELLS) for Wales and the Council for the Curriculum, Examinations and Assessment (CCEA) for Northern Ireland. The certificate may be accepted by Further Education institutions as proof of eligibility for attendance at higher level courses. Contact ie@padi.co.uk for an application form.

Europe

Divers have received credit for PADI courses in mainland Europe academic institutions and through the military; but since there is no formal recognition process, these have been individual cases. For more information or for a specific request, contact PADI EMEA at training.emea@padi.com.

Japan

Those who want to teach diving in Japanese school systems (colleges, universities, vocational schools, etc.) undergo general and specialized course work and testing to become authorized by the Japan Sports Association (JASA), under the jurisdiction of the Ministry of Education, Culture, Sports, Science and Technology. PADI Open Water Scuba Instructors are exempt from this specialized course and test, and can attain JASA authorization by taking a general course and certification test. For more information go to www.japan-sports.or.jp.

New Zealand

PADI Divers may qualify to receive recognition through a New Zealand Qualification Authority accredited provider. Open Water Diver, Advanced Open Water Diver and Rescue Diver qualify for the National Certificate of Diving: Foundational Skills; Divemasters and Open Water Scuba Instructors qualify for the National Certificate of Diving: Leadership; and Specialty Instructors qualify for the National Certificate of Diving: Instruction. For more information, go to www.padi.com/scuba/scuba-diving-guide/start-scuba-diving/scuba-lessons-for-college-credit/default.aspx.

United States

The American Council on Education's College Credit Recommendation Service (ACE CREDIT) has evaluated and recommended college credit for 16 PADI courses, and the EFR Instructor course. The American Council on Education, the major coordinating body for all the nation's higher education institutions, seeks to provide leadership and a unifying voice on key higher education issues and to influence public policy through advocacy, research, and program initiatives. For more information on ACE CREDIT recommendations, and to order an official PADI transcript, go to www.padi.com/scuba/scuba-diving-guide/start-scuba-diving/scuba-lessons-for-college-credit/default.aspx or contact PADI Americas at training@padi.com.

Where will your PADI certification take you next?

DISCOVER MORE. EXPLORE MORE. SAVE MORE.